Painted with traditional patterns, an Aborigine waits to dance at a ritual in Australia's Kimberley region. Eleven million acres here belong to Aboriginal communities through freehold or leasehold.

BEYOND THE
HORIZON

Adventures in Faraway Lands

Prepared by the Book Division
National Geographic Society, Washington, D.C.

BEYOND THE HORIZON
Adventures in Faraway Lands

Contributing Authors: Patrick R. Booz,
Christine Eckstrom, Tom Melham, Thomas O'Neill,
Cynthia Russ Ramsay

Contributing Photographers: Jeffrey Aaronson, Paul Chesley,
Jay Dickman, Maggie Steber

Published by The National Geographic Society
John M. Fahey, Jr., *President and Chief Executive Officer*
Gilbert M. Grosvenor, *Chairman of the Board*
Nina D. Hoffman, *Senior Vice President*

Prepared by The Book Division
William R. Gray, *Vice President and Director*
Charles Kogod, *Assistant Director*
Barbara A. Payne, *Editorial Director and Managing Editor*

Staff for this Special Publication
Toni Eugene, *Managing Editor*
John G. Agnone, *Illustrations Editor*
Jody Bolt, *Art Director*
Susan C. Eckert, Victoria D. Garrett, *Researchers*
Alice Jablonsky, *Contributing Researcher*
Patrick R. Booz, Richard M. Crum, Edward Lanouette,
Tom Melham, Cynthia Russ Ramsay, *Picture Legend Writers*
Carl Mehler, Joseph F. Ochlak, Isaac Ortiz,
Martin S. Walz, *Map Art, Production, and Research*
Sandra F. Lotterman, *Editorial Assistant*
Karen Dufort Sligh, *Illustrations Assistant*
Heather Guwang, *Production Project Manager*
Lewis R. Bassford, H. Robert Morrison, Richard S. Wain,
Production
Karen F. Edwards, Elizabeth G. Jevons,
Artemis S. Lampathakis, Teresita Cóquia Sison,
Marilyn J. Williams, *Staff Assistants*

Manufacturing and Quality Management
George V. White, *Director;* John T. Dunn, *Associate Director;*
Vincent P. Ryan, *Manager;* and R. Gary Colbert

Elisabeth MacRae-Bobynskyj, *Indexer*

*PRECEDING PAGES: Steaming earth cloaks a sunset
vista from atop Kverkfjöll, a mountain in central Iceland.
Below the climbers spreads an arm of Vatnajökull,
one of the world's largest ice fields.*

*Monks in training, two novices study Buddhist
prayers outside the rebuilt prayer hall of Muli Monastery
in southwestern China.*

*FOLLOWING PAGES: Market day draws lively crowds
in Kani Kombolé, a Dogon village east
of the Niger River in Mali.*

Foreword

Before dawn on a sultry day a few years ago, I hiked through long grass toward a broad swath of roily water. I paused at the edge and waited while the African sun slowly ignited a scene magical not only in its reality but also in the way it fulfilled my imagination. I watched transfixed as the two arms of a fabled river—one flowing from distant, deserted highlands, the other from verdant, misty mountains— merged to form the Nile, longest river in the world. For more than 25 years, I had dreamed of this scene, imagining time and again the confluence of the Blue Nile and the White Nile. I had read the accounts of John Hanning Speke and Richard Burton, of David Livingstone and Henry Morton Stanley, and of the many other adventurers who had explored the Nile seeking its elusive source.

Later that day I ambled through the dusty streets of the city of Khartoum, which hugs the Nile. At every turn I was jostled by noisy merchants, tense-faced dervishes, haughty camels. I thought of the British general Charles "Chinese" Gordon and the Mahdi—the Muslim messiah—who had struggled fiercely for control of the city in the 1880s, and I thought of the centuries of history that had gone before. Again, reality and years of thinking and wondering mingled in a confluence as tangible as that of the two branches of the Nile.

Khartoum, the Nile. The very names evoke romance, adventure, excitement—and such names make maps come alive. When I was a boy, my father and I papered my bedroom walls with maps. I'd study them by the hour and dream of places with names like Papeete, Serengeti, Little Diomede, Tasmania, Easter Island. I have been fortunate in my career at the National Geographic Society to have explored these and many other alluring locales and to have written of my experiences in the pages of Society books.

Like you, I look forward to being transported to new and exciting places in this volume. The remote and haunting *tepuís* of Venezuela have always been a magnet to me—but I have never had the opportunity to venture there. The words and photographs of that chapter, though, make me feel as if I have, for they truly capture the precipitous, mist-filled essence of that primordial place.

Likewise, I can hear the hushed chants and the delicate tinkling of bells in the Buddhist temples of the Muli region of China. I can feel the sturdy gait of a diminutive Icelandic horse on a cross-country trip into the interior of that land of sprawling glaciers punctuated by geysers and volcanoes. I can mingle in the dusty crowds of a village market near the brown waters of the Niger River in Mali. And I can face ferocious crocodiles thrashing in a muddy backwater in the sun-washed Kimberley region of Australia.

Place-names from other maps that papered the walls of my boyhood bedroom beckon to me from these chapters—Angel Falls, Timor Sea, Timbuktu. I have not visited these places yet, but if I do, I know my years of imagining them will combine with the reality there to provide a compelling, rewarding experience of discovery.

As I have been, I hope that you will be enthralled by the stories and images in this book as, together, we explore five enchanted realms beyond the horizon.

WILLIAM R. GRAY
Director, Book Division

In late afternoon Río Carrao mirrors a sunlit ledge of Auyan-tepui,
a mesa-like mountain in southeastern Venezuela.

JAY DICKMAN

CHINA

THE KINGDOM OF MULI

Great changes have swept the mountainous and wild border region of China and Tibet that was long an independent Buddhist kingdom; yet many traditions endure.

By Patrick R. Booz   Photographed by Jeffrey Aaronson

O ut of the misty silence the world erupts with sound. Huge conch shells send deep boomings across the mountain valley. The ceremony starts. Two rows of monks enter and sit with quick discipline, though the young ones have a glint of mischief in their eyes. The old monks, shrouded in maroon robes, settle beneath altar statues and silk banners. The scene, visually rich, is soon transformed by sound. Bells trill, hand drums ripple . . . then chanting takes over. It rises and falls, picks up force like rolling thunder, carries, then descends to a low, melancholy minor key. Clapping abruptly halts the chanting. Slowly, a single monk, benign and composed, closes his eyes, centers himself in concentration, and begins a weird, double-echoic song, known musicologically as overtone chanting. Whatever its name, the phenomenon is eerie and penetrating. His voice, multiplied as through a sonic prism, shakes the temple to its very timbers.

The monk stops chanting, and the abbot strides forward. He is gloriously robed in multiple layers of colorful cotton and silk brocade and wears on his bald head the high, arched, fringed headdress of Tibet's Yellow Hat Buddhists. He carries a heavy, four-sided scepter inlaid with silver. It crashes down to signal the start of a stern sermon. The abbot exhorts the young monks in their studies, scolds them for misdemeanors, then ends with a blessing. His severe face softens for a moment. The ceremony is over; like puppies, the youngsters pour out into the courtyard, and the spell is broken.

I emerged with the monks and blinked in the daylight. After a decade of knowing about this place, of dreaming about it, I was truly here in Muli. Ten years before, I had been an English teacher in Yunnan Province to the south, where I heard beguiling tales about this land and its monastic traditions. I felt lucky to speak Mandarin Chinese, the lingua franca

Faces and costumes distinctive and varied reflect the cultural diversity of the Muli region of China's Sichuan Province, near Tibet. This Yi woman left the mountains to work in a logging camp.

PRECEDING PAGES: Beyond Muli Monastery, morning mist shrouds the limestone steeps of Jyakwen Sera. Tibetans have lived in the Muli region since the seventh century.

throughout China's distant reaches, and I knew it would serve me well here. This monastery once stood at the heart of the kingdom of Muli, a remote domain about the size of Massachusetts tucked away in giant mountains along the Tibet-China border. Muli had existed in a state of de facto independence for more than 700 years, too far and too isolated from both Lhasa and Beijing to fall under the domination of either capital. Muli entered the modern world in the 1950s, as China steadily encroached and finally subdued this proud realm in a black wave of destruction during 1959–1960. Foreign travelers have always been few here—botanists, mountaineers, adventurers—and only a trickle had entered in the past 40 years.

The story of Muli really begins with the arrival of the Mongol warrior Kublai Khan and his conquest of southwest China in the 13th century. It is a tale of valor and success, and it changed Muli forever. Kublai's brother Mangu became the Great Khan in 1251. He had long desired to vanquish southern China's Sung Dynasty to bring the vast wealth of the Chinese empire under Mongol control, and he felt the time was ripe to act. Rather than attacking solely from the north, Mangu envisioned a masterful assault from the west as well. First, however, the independent Dali Kingdom, based in today's Yunnan Province, would have to fall, and here is where Kublai Khan strides onto the stage of world history.

Up to this point in his life, Kublai had had no experience in leading the swift, terrifying Mongolian cavalry or, indeed, as a warrior. He was in his mid-thirties, old to begin; his brothers and cousins had earned their fighting reputations in their teens. So when Mangu's orders came—subdue the Dali Kingdom, make it a base against the Sung, and open up trade with Burma and other parts of Southeast Asia—Kublai planned meticulously for his mission.

A swift southward march through formidable terrain in September 1253 brought Kublai to Muli. This wild land, where aboriginal people walked about with bows and arrows stuck in their loincloths, clearly needed controlling. Kublai installed one of his trusted officials as the local ruler. This man was the great-grandfather of Muli's first king, and his investiture marked the start of the kingdom of Muli. I was to see and hear more of the Great Khan later, and to realize how strong the memory of him remains in these parts.

The second great event in Muli's history was the arrival in 1580 of an ecclesiastic from Lhasa, a disciple of the Third Dalai Lama. He must have been a remarkably charismatic monk, able to heal and to perform miracles. Within a few years he converted most of Muli to the Yellow Hat sect, the "reformed" branch of Buddhism that stresses monastic discipline and a steady, gradual, moral path to wisdom and enlightenment. His revitalized monasteries stood at the heart of Muli's life and formed the focus of its culture.

In 1924 one of this century's most eccentric and capable explorers, an Austro-American named Joseph Rock, entered Muli, befriended its king, and studied its institutions and geography. Rock found a kingdom with no towns, only monasteries, unchanged for hundreds of years. Of 18 religious centers, 3 were large—Muli, Kulu, and Waerhdje. Together they shared the seat of government in an endless, yearly rotation whereby the king and his court spent 12 months at each place in turn.

Muli, which gave its name to the whole kingdom, was the largest center, with 700 monks; Kulu housed perhaps 300; and Waerhdje, the oldest monastery in Muli, had 270. My purpose in coming to China was to visit each of the three main monasteries and see what, if anything, remained after the destruction of 1959–1960. My visits would involve a lot of traveling, and I braced myself for the weeks ahead.

For now, though, I was content simply to be at Muli, alive, breathing well in the thin air of the 10,000-foot elevation, and sharing this moment of elation on a distant, forgotten mountainside. My traveling companion was Jeffrey Aaronson, a remarkably energetic and dedicated photographer. We had journeyed for four days by jeep from Chengdu, capital of southwest China's Sichuan Province. Most of the way was on execrable roads, difficult at any time of year, but downright forbidding now that the rainy season had begun. Again and again we saw the remains of horrible accidents, real-life enactments of the hand-painted warning signs posted along the roadside: trucks and jeeps in midair, flying upside down into the gorges below. Deep mud was always a problem. Stuck for the umpteenth time, I was reminded of the tart Chinese saying, "Roads: good for ten years, bad for ten thousand."

At one such interminable wait I saw Tibetan truckers for the first time, hard, dignified men who carried their faith, literally, in their truck cabs. The interiors were plastered from roof to floor with pictures and posters of the Buddha, the Goddess of Mercy, sages, and Tibet's formidable-looking deities. Small altars rested on the dashboards. These new Tibetan nomads, roaring down from the mountains with their loads of lumber, epitomize the changes that have come to Muli since the 1950s. Once it was thought that gold from the rushing rivers would be the resource to open this land. In fact it has been the vast timbered forests—described to me by a local as Muli's "new gold"—that have brought change and dislocation.

The very roads Jeffrey and I traversed were built by loggers to push farther and farther into the interior. The influx—these men, their families, the truck drivers and mechanics, the mill workers, the forestry officials, the technicians and scientists, the road maintenance crews—has forever altered the demography of Muli. Before 1950 virtually no Chinese lived here. Now Chinese and Tibetans each comprise about 30 percent of the population, and the remaining 40 percent is an assortment of wildly varied minority peoples—Yi, Miao, Naxi, Zhuang, Lisu, Bai, and Pumi.

Logging towns and outposts were everywhere, shambling, ugly communities that reminded me of pictures of rough-and-tumble gold-rush towns of the Yukon at the turn of the century. A single dirt street passed dry-goods stores, cigarette stalls with bars on the windows, stacks of firewood, scattered piles of tubers for food. Flea-ridden dogs ambled around.

Seeing these changes heightened my eagerness to reach the monastic sites and discover the remnants of a fast-disappearing way of life. I was reminded of Joseph Rock's articles in NATIONAL GEOGRAPHIC, unique records of China's frontier regions. He described Muli in 1925 as "one of the least-known spots in the world."

In one of Rock's old photographs, taken from a distance across the Muli River Valley, the Muli Monastery is a white oval floating in space. The boundary of that oval was once a high, white wall that completely enclosed the lama-city of myriad whitewashed buildings. When I arrived in Muli, the wall was down; only hummocks of rubble remained. And within that broken boundary, every single structure was leveled in 1959. A few monks were spared, the rest were killed or dispersed.

Today the two main structures have been rebuilt at the lowest and highest limits of the former monastery. The lower building, the Tsugyeng, is the principal hall and home for old and new works of art. No sculpture survived the destruction of the 1950s and '60s, a tragedy considering the exceptional quality of the works; but a dozen valuable *thankas* remain, elaborate painted silk scrolls portraying deities, historical figures, and legendary cities.

On a door I looked closely at a thanka print. It bore in English the following prayer, which poignantly sums up the storm of horror that covered Tibet in recent decades: "May this thanka provide protection from danger in the present Age of Darkness."

The upper palace, known as Chira, was once the most sacred shrine of Muli; today it is a modest chapel, though its setting is sublime—on a dressed-stone terrace amid flowers and fruit trees, flanked by small, neat cells for the senior lamas.

Reconstruction has occurred only in the last several years, and it continues. The smell of new wood permeates the grounds as sawyers—local villagers who give time and labor freely—sweat and strain with formidable two-man saws. The gaudy paint, the volunteers erecting new quarters by the tamped-earth method of wall building, the bustle of monks, all point to a resurgence of faith. The effort, the cooperation, and the obvious devotion in all this activity moved me.

Compromises are necessary to reduce costs. The temple roofs once glimmered with real gold. As I watched, however, a young monk on a rickety ladder sloshed yellow paint across the tiles. This is the "gold" of Muli's contemporary roofs.

Early one morning I found that the whole community of monks had gathered at the wooded edge of the grounds. They carried baskets of greens, bundles of twigs, churns for tea, bags of barley flour, rugs, a caldron, and oversize cooking utensils. Most intriguing of all were various carefully guarded boxes, repositories for religious objects. Everyone was in high spirits over a daylong picnic ahead, though the reason for the outing—as well as its focus—was a sacred ritual of blessing and thanksgiving. The celebration of Zhe-re-yeh was a movable feast, literally; it had to be performed in the dark, watery recesses of the monastery's sacred mountain, Jyakwen Sera, home of its protective deity.

"We go up to the mountain," explained a monk named Tsering, "to honor the spirits of the water and their special abode, the stream we call Nyenku. This stream originates inside the holy mountain; its waters nourish our crops and allow us to drink. It is clean, delicious water! And of course the cold water helps wash away the impurity in our lives."

I followed the procession as it climbed higher and higher through deepening forests, past cliffs entangled with wild roses and rhododendrons, into the limestone defile of Jyakwen Sera. High above the trail impossibly situated caves stared down at us. These were the monastery's hermit retreats, aeries of the anchorites.

The monks finally made camp at a tiny clearing dominated by the roar of tumbling water. The little ones set about erecting a colorful blue-and-white tent and gaily collecting wood for the fire. All the while their songs wove in and out of nature's own chorus of wind and rapids and the cries of birds in the mist.

As time approached for the ceremony, to be carried on deeper still inside the mountain's embrace, the group grew serious. I was told forthrightly that this was no longer a place for me. A middle-aged monk, slightly bent and reminiscent of a mythic wizard, came toward me with a sympathetic smile and put his hand on my shoulder. "When you become a monk, you can join us."

Encouraged by the spirit of the monks—by the fact that they still conduct secret ceremonies—I was eager to seek out and explore the kingdom of Muli's second great monastery. It used to take three days to travel from Muli to Kulu on foot. Even today the road is bad; it climbs steeply for hours through pine and rhododendron forests, and finally peters out just below the tree line.

Once, along the way, I was transported backward in time. Beyond a rise, three mounted horsemen, hunters from afar, raced through a celestial field of grazing yaks. The men bellowed and laughed and were happy to show off their fearlessness and their rifles. When I asked about Kulu, they shrugged and waved me off. Perhaps its name was all that remained of the monastery.

Eventually, a battered track opened onto a series of alpine meadows. In the distance, beyond a line of prayer flags, lay Kulu Monastery—ruins silhouetted against a brooding black sky. The beauty and the sadness of the vision pulled me up short. From the Muli king's palace bleak sections of wall stuck up like the ribs of a giant carcass.

I hurried to the long, low chanting halls, smashed and battered beyond recognition. A forlorn entranceway still stood, its wooden, lion-headed gargoyles faded and choked with

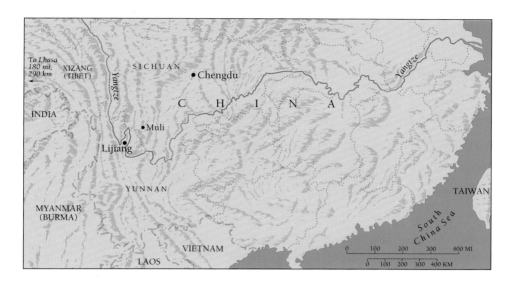

Remote reaches of western China near Muli Monastery remain a land of mystery.

moss. Inside the courtyard a bronze censer four feet across lay skewed in the mud. It served as an animal trough.

My search for people turned up two herders, Jamyang Trashi and his friend, both 18 years old. Only their families lived in Kulu, they told me; the monks had gone long before the two boys were born.

I took out photographs of Kulu Monastery when it still thrived, and the boys crowded to my side. Although they lacked any formal education, they asked penetrating questions about the past, about Tibetan religion, about the old ways.

On the way back from Kulu, Jeffrey and I were trapped in a hellish rainstorm. We pressed against an earthen embankment but found little protection. Vulnerable, like the monastery itself, we watched the ruins slowly disappear in the gathering gloom.

Upon returning to Muli Monastery, I found a band of monks planting trees. They had chosen carefully the site for the arbor-to-be and were joyfully digging, tamping, measuring, and watering. These acts, full of hope, spoke clearly about the fledgling monastery's expectations for survival, a complete contrast to the defeat I had sadly witnessed at Kulu.

At dusk one day I glanced up the hill toward the chanting hall and happened to see the abbot being assisted by a mountain girl. She carried his cloth bag and a long log for the hearth fire effortlessly. I approached cautiously and engaged the abbot first. Slowly I learned that the girl, 17 years old, was a distant relative from the region of Shulu, many days away on foot. She was making a round of pilgrimages. Wary, attentive, skittish, she reminded me of a wild animal. She felt safe next to the old lama, but she avoided everyone else. In her hair she wore large studs of turquoise; around her neck roseate glass beads caught the hues of her lips and cheeks. A broad ivory bangle was pushed firmly up one forearm. Beneath her beauty lay an unmistakable layer of grime—clearly she never washed—that accentuated her wildness. She belonged to another age.

Such people excited Joseph Rock and inspired his work. His scientific mind, eye for detail, and scholarly enthusiasm led him far and wide to record indigenous cultures and tracts of untrammeled nature. His magnum opus, *The Ancient Na-khi Kingdom of Southwest China,* presented his findings with mind-numbing exactness. Most of it is for specialists, but entries intriguing to laymen do pop up. Rock vividly describes the gorges where three of Asia's mightiest rivers—the Salween, Mekong, and Yangtze—flow through cavernous, parallel trenches, all separated by a mere hundred miles. He tells of Medicine Mountain, a strange 15,000-foot massif covered with medicinal worms, herbs, and roots. And then there is his description of the Boneless Pig.

In preparation for my trip, I was astonished to see a photograph—taken by Rock along the Yunnan-Sichuan border—of a gigantic sow, devoid of limbs and oddly flattened, taller than the men supporting it. The caption described a "Boneless Pig: They are often kept for ten years, and are used for mattresses for that length of time, before being eaten." Now, in the 1990s, did people still sleep on pig-mattresses? Did they eat decade-old sections of pork fat? Did this tradition survive the changes in China over the past 60 years?

Wondrously, it did—in Muli Monastery. A monk named Dili, only 11 years old, had become my friend and informant about daily activities. His care that I see and understand his life made him attentive to my every wish. I described the phenomenon of the pig, and he cried out, "The lama across the courtyard, he has one under his bed!"

It took me some time to convince the kind and doddering old lama that I really wanted to see his pig. Finally he and Dili scrabbled around on the floor, using a crooked walking stick to haul the porker out from under the bed. It was not as large as I had hoped, but a healthy three-foot-long specimen nevertheless. I whooped with the rush of discovery, and then we all laughed and laughed at the spectacle I made: an American adoring a hairy, squishy pig that had been resting for years under a lama's bed. When the laughter subsided, the dear old monk turned to me and apologized that his pig was too small to sleep on.

I learned more about boneless pigs directly below the monastery in the village of Nyi-i-dyen, a peaceful, prosperous community rife with grubby, happy children and alive with the sounds of their games. Walnut and apple trees bowered each sturdy stone house, and shaded paths led outward to the fields. I followed one of the trails and found a herder lying in a pasture, head under an umbrella, languorously looking after his family's cattle, milk cows, sheep, and goats. Tashi was his name, and we fell to talking.

"How is a boneless pig prepared?" I asked intently.

"Well, it's a bit complex. First you need a good fat pig; we usually get ours ready for the New Year. Then you slaughter it . . . gently." Tashi passed a finger across his neck slowly. "Open it up lengthwise, take out the innards, and then use a very sharp knife to remove all the bones. The spine is especially hard to get out. Leave a little meat and as much fat as possible. Preserve it with lots and lots of salt, and sew the old thing up! You have to be careful, though. We once had one that puffed up and nearly exploded. Come on, I'll show you some boneless pigs—all the houses around here have two or three."

Tashi, a lamb under one arm, drove his animals home with shouts and gestures. His handsome, burly brother Tenzing, clearly a stalwart of the village, greeted us. They soon had two boneless pigs up against a wall for my review. Tashi tapped the skull of one and explained, "That's the only bone we leave behind. We cut away the jaw bones so the pig's chin will lie flat, but the hard skull keeps the shape of the face. We like that."

Tashi's mother entered, and I asked her about pig-mattresses.

"No, in these parts we don't sleep on them anymore. You have to go farther south for that," she said, digging her elbow into a plump, four-and-a-half-foot porker. "But we do lean against them when we're tired." We settled down for a long afternoon of tea, boneless-pig soup, and roast boneless pig.

A final incident at Muli Monastery reinforced my conviction that it will endure. One evening after supper, I cocked an ear to clamorous chanting going on up the hill and decided to make a close inspection. Near the upper hall I chanced upon the aged, beneficent lama who chanted in the astounding, double-toned way. He seemed the archetypal Tibetan mystic, wrapped in his robes, sitting in the lotus position, serene and imperturbable. This evening he was helping the novices.

Those youngsters, ranging in age from 8 to 18, clustered on the chanting-hall porch each evening like a band of monkeys, playful yet purposeful. They came to practice reading and chanting. Reciting from long leaves of woodblock-printed scriptures, some shouted at the top of their lungs, others raced along chattering syllables to show off. The slower ones mouthed each word, stumbled, then started over. These last ones scurried to the feet of the kindly lama for help when faced with a particularly difficult section.

In the soft light of candles, the sage's eyes and voice encouraged. He leaned close and whispered—prompting—until a passage was successfully pronounced. Every pupil was finally dismissed with a loving pat on the head.

Patient, radiating care for each little soul, the attentive master clearly aimed to nurture the tradition of Tibetan Buddhism through these eager boys. They will uphold the tradition when he is gone.

A Joseph Rock photograph published in 1931 remains a valuable record of Waerhdje Monastery, oldest of all Muli's 18 religious centers. The picture, taken from a thousand feet above the 10,500-foot-high monastery, shows the 400-year-old chanting halls, the king's palace, chapels, the dozens of smaller cells, workshops, and refectories. Far below, snaking southward into the ranks of limitless mountains, is the Muli River. The panorama is one of impressive grandeur, and Waerhdje seems a secure and permanent part of the landscape. I longed to see what remained of it some 60 years after Rock's visit.

It would be a tiring ascent, so I arranged for horses to carry Jeffrey, me, and our equipment. Our guide turned out to be the best possible friend for the next three days—capable, robust, buoyant—a man of deep and simple happiness. His name was Japa, and his alertness to the world delighted me. Here, I thought, is a human who really lives.

This Tibetan had suffered badly at the hands of the Chinese, yet his small face and ever-twinkling eyes, offset by comically large ears, never betrayed any bitterness or defeat. Jeffrey and I wobbled on our little ponies as Japa led us upward, telling us stories as we went. Across the Muli River Valley to the west was an entire terraced mountainside covered with crops—mauve, umber, pale green, pink, olive.

"The pink, that's buckwheat in bloom," said Japa. "In the olden days we used to pay our taxes in buckwheat." As a form of tribute to China, Muli each year sent buckwheat 150 miles to Yanyuan, the closest Chinese-controlled center.

Our little caravan wound slowly through pine forests along the old pilgrim trail to the monastery. Prayer flags, carved stone images of the Buddha, and religious cairns known as *latses* punctuated the route. One outstanding, painstakingly constructed latse of great girth and solidity stood 12 feet high. It was topped by a slate slab, and this in turn was surmounted by white crystalline rocks. What care and devotion had gone into it!

"Who built this?" I asked in wonder.

Japa looked at the ground, then at the sky, and finally shot me a playful glance. "I did," he said. "It took me a year."

The approach to Waerhdje skirted a field of tall, black-and-white prayer flags. Their rustling heightened the thrill of arrival. A gnomic lama, round-faced, wrinkled, wearing a knitted cap and mincing along in high, faded felt boots, emerged from a low stone hut. He greeted us sweetly and soon began telling us his life's tale.

"My name is Lobsang Trashi," he said. "I've lived on this mountain for more than 70 years, so being a monk is all I know. Oh, I did travel once, long, long ago, all the way to Lhasa, where I studied."

When I asked how he got to Lhasa, more than 700 air miles away, Lobsang Trashi straightened his back, marched in place, and for an instant regained his youth.

"A long walk!" he beamed.

A quick calculation showed Lobsang Trashi had made his epic pilgrimage in 1929. He slowly grew solemn and told us how the army had ravaged Waerhdje in 1959. Only two monks and Japa lived among the ruins of this formerly glorious site.

The vehemence of the destruction here can be attributed in part to Waerhdje's rank as the oldest, most venerable institution in Muli. The monastery's most beautiful temple contained a five-foot-tall gold-and-jeweled masterpiece that represented a special image of the Buddha—the Jo statue. The Jokhang—the temple that housed the statue—and the Jo itself have vanished, thoroughly obliterated.

Japa ended this somber moment with his irrepressible optimism.

"Don't worry," he said. "I'm going to rebuild that Jokhang. Look what I have done already."

He showed me to a tall, narrow building, the *donkar*. It housed a single item, an immense prayer wheel, ten feet high, crudely painted in bright yellow, green, red, and blue. This ingenious folk-art contraption, built of beaten metal, gears, and rods salvaged from a logging camp, again showed Japa's resourcefulness. It serves as a focus for pilgrims, who come to turn the wheel as a way of acquiring religious merit. Inside the drum are scriptures, and each revolution sends anthems of prayers heavenward.

Now it was time for refreshment and rest, instructed Japa. He led me by the hand up a steep wooden stairway into his kitchen. This dark, smoke-filled room was the center of all activity—hearth, dining room, living room, and playroom. In 1929 Kermit and Ted Roosevelt, sons of President Theodore Roosevelt, passed near here while on a hunting trip. They noted that "the houses in Muli have no chimneys," and that "the smoke was suffocating." I agreed. Billows from the fire made me weep and streamed out the small windows.

"Teatime!" Japa announced. Even this gloomy room grew cheerful with his presence.

Tea for Tibetans is serious business. When dry, it is a primary item for sale or barter. Prepared to drink, it provides hydration and stimulus at high elevations and is the focus of happy social gatherings.

Japa, ever active, moved to his "tea corner," site of the paraphernalia for preparation. The tea was in the form of a pressed, one-pound brick. Sections could be broken off and crumbled as needed. Yak butter lay in a delicate woven basket. A carved wooden tub held salt, and next to it was a lidded box with soda ash, which helps the ingredients mix. Finally, to impart a taste especially favored here in Muli, there were ground marijuana seeds in a shallow pan. A miniature grinder stood nearby to turn a bag of seeds into the requisite paste. Japa boiled the tea in water, put it and the other ingredients into a churn, and beat the mixture into a fragrant, frothy soup.

Tea, and more tea, drunk with honor out of classic high-based, broad-rimmed Tibetan bowls, preceded and followed a simple but filling meal. We drank to thank Japa for his hospitality. He had given us everything he had—food, shelter, friendship.

We retired early. Japa gave me his bed, and Jeffrey slept on a pallet in Japa's guest bedroom—his private chapel. Its altar held a dazzling collection of statuary and offerings: clay tablets, butter sculptures, tea, liquor, biscuits, beads, paintings. Japa came in to light the oil lamps and found Jeffrey already zipped into his sleeping bag. Our Tibetan host clearly found this a novel way to sleep. "What a sight!" he laughed. "He's become a caterpillar!"

After a moment Japa turned to me. "By the way, there are little . . . things . . . here, just this big," he said, pinching the tip of his index finger. "They suck blood, but you don't need to worry about them."

"You mean lice," I said.

"That's right. But never mind, they only come down from the ceiling when it rains." It had been pouring steadily for six hours.

From my own little window I said goodnight to the flowing mountains that rolled away, wave upon wave, into the enormous, wet night. I felt my smallness and isolation, and I wondered about friends and family and the outside world. Rummaging through debris on the sill, I discovered that Japa kept an archaic shortwave radio. I flicked it on. It still worked, and I scanned the band. Out of the purple darkness, in this awesome landscape on the edge of Tibet, came: "and now for Wimbledon lawn tennis." The world was still out there. I quickly snapped the radio off.

The time came to say good-bye to Japa. He accompanied us down to the pilgrim path, joking, encouraging, commenting on the flowers. Finally he let us go with shouts and waves. "Come back, come back one day!" As we descended on foot, I wondered if ever again I would see that rare and happy man.

We left not just Japa but Muli itself in a light drizzle, eager to pick up again the trail of Kublai Khan. Our path southward to the Yunnan-Sichuan border area passed through a swath of territory inhabited by the Yi, a minority people who range over five of China's provinces. They number more than five million, with many subgroups and dialects.

As we crossed the Mofagou Mountains, a bad patch of road stopped us. High in the hills, from crags and boulders, came eerie voices. We saw no one. Then slowly, carefully, one by one, a gang of boys descended, all with antique rifles and fierce dogs. They were dressed in leather and dirt, as if born from the very hills themselves. These were genuine mountain Yi, who live a life of great ruggedness and independence. Hunting, combined with agriculture, sustains them.

Fields of potatoes filled narrow valleys with pale white blossoms, some patches growing on 55-degree slopes. Corn, the other major crop of the Yi, is used to create a powerful, brain-whacking distilled brew that they love, and love to introduce to guests. True peril awaits anyone who gets involved in a Yi drinking session!

The houses along this stretch of the frontier are log cabins, huddled together in little groups, insignificant in the mountains' vastness. An uplifting decorative touch relieves the harsh architecture. Just below the eaves a strip of luminous light blue runs up to the roof crest and down again. I asked about this one piece of color. It represents, I found, the sky—heaven itself—just above the heads of the people. Its freshness was indeed heavenly, its presence, a constant reminder of the celestial world to come.

In these villages, Yi men invariably dress in dark colors; the older ones, tall and proud, wear indigo turbans and long, black tunics.

The women are a different matter altogether. Amazing, arousing Yi maidens wear full-length, pleated skirts banded horizontally with every hue of the rainbow. Elaborate, outsize jewelry—floral silver earrings and metallic neck-brooches that resemble radiators—shimmer above their jerkins and vests. All Yi women in this region wear ornate headdresses. A rigid frame forms the base for a rectangular platform of black cloth that spreads to the width of the women's shoulders. Embroidery, double-layering, finials, and appliqué decorate the platform. These baroque canopies give a regal air to even the simplest mountain girl.

In a small market Jeffrey stopped to take photographs. His mere presence sent a crowd of young women into a panic of retreat. Their slender bodies, turning quickly in unison, resembled a flurry of peacocks; their skirts whooshed like a flock of doves.

After two days we reached Lugu Lake, a beautiful body of water that straddles the Yunnan-Sichuan border. We first stayed on the Sichuan side in the strange village of Zuosuo, a Babel where the children routinely speak three or four tongues—Moso, Tibetan, Mandarin, Pumi. The peculiarity of this place, its unfamiliar architecture, its cautious inhabitants, became understandable when I found out that it was a rare enclave of Bon, the archaic, pre-Buddhist religion of Tibet that relies heavily on sorcery. Magic abounded in Zuosuo.

On a hillside loomed a bizarre structure, a complicated tower with a central axis or "mast" embellished like the Christmas tree of a madman. The top of the tower, 18 feet above the ground, held a wooden offering tablet painted with a divinity surrounded by a green halo. Below it was a rampage of twine, wire, and yarn, both scrambled and coherent, like a damaged spiderweb. Amid the jumble hung many tablets and cloth ties of varied colors.

The entire tower was a classic *nya-ta,* a demon trap to disarm evil forces and negate maledictions. Overlooking the crop fields, it was also meant to prevent devastating hail.

In Zuosuo's Bon temple I saw a carefully carved, four-sided piece of wood, a "charm stick," with many incised gods, deities, animals, and humanlike representations of diseases and natural forces.

With a shudder we left Zuosuo. We drove around Lugu Lake, entered Yunnan Province, and moved on to the end of our travels. On the plain of Yongning, 20 miles west of Lugu Lake, Kublai Khan massed his forces before the decisive battle against the Dali Kingdom. At a place called Ri Yue He, "the union of sun and moon," he camped. I climbed the steep hill of La-ba-drr to see the famous meadow below, now a field of corn, rice, and tobacco. Local octogenarians recounted with toothless smiles that the Great Khan made the same climb to view his troops. The scene was spectacular, the vantage strategically incomparable.

To the east rose Lion Mountain, a living presence on the plain—dominant, inescapable, its moods shifting with the slightest alteration in light. To the north the purple ranges of Sichuan rose ever higher as they mounted to Muli and Tibet. Verdant fields crisscrossed with irrigation channels splayed in all directions, and to the northeast lay Yongning, little more than an overgrown village with a single, arrow-straight street.

Directly below me was the former campground and garrison of the Mongols, bisected by a stream that from these heights was a silent, silver ribbon. For centuries after Kublai Khan camped here with his troops, anyone starting a journey from Yongning camped here first.

Conjuring visions of noise and dust, of a thousand neighing horses and the bannered ranks of Mongol warriors, I turned slowly to gaze southward. There a red road cut from the clay hills wound upward to a green pass in the far mountains. This was the very route that Kublai Khan followed; beyond the pass flowed the Upper Yangtze, known here as the River of Golden Sand, site of his ultimate victory. I longed to go there on foot myself, to breathe hard and never look back, to leave this point of grand departures—but that journey would have to wait for another time.

Together, a Miao family struggles to scratch a living from the narrow Muli River Valley. Chinese-style clothing has replaced the traditional garb of the Miao, one of many minority peoples in the Muli area.

FOLLOWING PAGES: Alone on a giant green staircase, a peasant weeds terraced fields of rice in the Xiangling River gorge. The young shoots flourish in the rains of early June.

*R*ising from ruins, the Tsugyeng—main assembly hall—of Muli Monastery stands anew on the site of the Muli king's palace. Once a monastic city of 700 devout Buddhists, the cloister was destroyed in 1959; it rebounds now with financial help from China's Buddhist Association. Blasts from a shell trumpet call the faithful to prayer. A freshly painted beam carries an injunction to all those who enter the hall. In Chinese and Tibetan it reminds: No Smoking! No Photography!

FOLLOWING PAGES: *Crackling flames heat a giant wok of water in the monastery kitchen, where a young monk waits to ready tea for a prayer service. A part of monastic life unchanged for centuries, the Tibetan kitchen features fire, smoke, outsize utensils, and traditional food.*

*N*oble in bearing, the abbot of Muli strides from the chanting hall at the close of a ceremony. A living link with Tsongkhapa, 15th-century founder of the sect, the abbot wears the symbol of Yellow Hat Buddhism when he conducts services.

*Y*outh aids age as a novice steadies an old monk in the courtyard of the rebuilt monastery of Muli. Peering from a cell, home for most of his 75 years, the patriarch (left) remembers the 1924 visit of explorer and botanist Joseph Rock, first foreign chronicler of the Muli kingdom; since then he has witnessed vast changes, including the arrival of Chinese rule in the late 1950s.

FOLLOWING PAGES: *Glowering clouds descend toward brooding mountains beyond Kulu Monastery, a thriving center of 300 monks until its destruction by Chinese forces in 1960. Fenced fields affirm the efforts of two surviving families that eke out an existence here at 12,000 feet.*

*A*fternoon drizzle accompanies Lobsang Trashi across flagstones of Waerhdje Monastery;
one of only three people living on the mountain, he keeps the flame of faith alive.

FOLLOWING PAGES: Forest of prayer flags edges the pilgrim path to Waerhdje Monastery
at dawn. Each flutter of woodblock-printed cloth sends a holy message heavenward.

Hunters from the hinterland, two Tibetans eye activities along the single street of a Sichuan town. A charm of twisted yarn bestows blessings on all who enter the home; common decorations throughout the Muli region, such colorful symbols summon good luck.

*B*earing a basket of offerings (opposite), a dugout canoe glides toward Anawa Island
in Lugu Lake, on the border of Yunnan and Sichuan Provinces. Atop the tiny, sacred isle (above),
local shaman He Yang each day ignites an offering of eucalyptus leaves and pine needles,
then prays as he circles the stone stupa, or shrine. Joseph Rock visited Lugu many times between
1924 and 1949; he lived for several months on one of five islands in the lake.

*S*erene for eternity, a three-foot-tall statue of Tsongkhapa (above), the founder of Yellow Hat Buddhism, gazes benignly from an elaborate framework of colored butter sculpture in the Yongning Lamasary. The town of Yongning lies in Yunnan, just south of the ancient kingdom of Muli. The abbot of Jade Summit Monastery outside the Yunnan city of Lijiang spins a silver prayer wheel as he chants and paces. Finely-crafted, pebbled courtyards remain a specialty of local Naxi builders.

FOLLOWING PAGES: Last light brushes the rooftops of Lijiang's Old Town, parts of which have changed little since Mongol emperor Kublai Khan conquered the area more than 700 years ago. Citizens of Lijiang still take pride in the fine woodwork and fired tiles of their buildings and the house plants that bring the natural world into their homes.

MALI

LANDS ALONG THE NIGER

*In Mali's arid grasslands south of the Sahara, a legendary
African river and fickle rains dominate the lives of diverse peoples
from Timbuktu to the cliffside villages of the Dogon.*

By Cynthia Russ Ramsay   Photographed by Maggie Steber

At midday a white glare plays harshly on the crumbling walls, corrugated tin doors, and streets silted with sand, throwing the city's withering decay into sharp relief. But by moonlight the mosques of mud and the pale, boxy houses possess a pearly luster, and the dusty collection of buildings is transformed into a realm of shimmer and shadow amid a sea of dunes that shine like molten silver.

On one such beguiling evening, the sinuous alleyways of this African city were almost deserted. Even the urchins with impudent smiles had departed. Now and then a donkey brayed; otherwise it was eerily quiet.

In silence I followed my guide into a small compound where a kerosene lamp cast an amber glow on the plump, ebony face of Fatimata Yatara, a sturdy woman seated on a mat with her two young children fast asleep beside her. By day Fatimata sells peanuts at a small stall. By night she divines the future by tossing a handful of cowrie shells again and again and reading their positions when they land.

Fatimata was a popular seer, and faith in her supernatural powers reflected the importance of magic here. An aura of mystery hung heavily in the air, like the sand and dust roiled up by harmattan winds from the Sahara.

And there was reason to expect strange encounters, for this was Timbuktu, the remote and fabled desert metropolis in the Sahel, the arid steppe lands on the southern rim of the Sahara. Long inaccessible to Westerners, the city has become synonymous with the earth's farthest reaches.

As early as the 16th century, accounts of its great riches, learning, and revelry made the city legendary in Europe. Travelers told tales of veiled nomad warriors and dark, sloe-eyed

*Foretelling the future, a seer in fabled Timbuktu, Mali, uses Koranic verses inscribed in sand.
To enhance his powers, he holds a talisman and prayer beads, tokens of faith in magic and Islam.*

PRECEDING PAGES: *Dusty streets speak little of Timbuktu's past glory. Once an African crossroads
where camel caravans met Niger River canoes, the city remains a symbol of remoteness and mystery.*

slaves; of Muslim scholars and wealthy merchants prospering on the caravan trade. Camels from Timbuktu arrived in towns along the North African coast laden with ivory, ostrich plumes, and gold. In the late 18th century this "infinite treasure" fired an outburst of exploration in search of the great crossroads of African trade.

The quest for the elusive city coincided with a push to solve the riddle of the Niger River. Although stretches of the river had been highways of commerce for medieval African empires, no one knew where the Niger went—whether it flowed into the Nile or the Congo, or instead disappeared into the sands of the Sahara. By 1830 explorers had traced its baffling course—a huge 2,600-mile arc through West Africa that ended in the Atlantic Ocean at the Gulf of Guinea.

Most Europeans seeking Timbuktu struck out across the Sahara. They were beset by tropical fevers, terrible heat, and marauding tribes. Of the dozens who attempted the journey in the century before 1870, only three—Scotsman Alexander Gordon Laing, Frenchman René Caillié, and German Heinrich Barth—reached Timbuktu for certain, and Laing was murdered by a Fulani tribesman on the way back to Morocco.

Today traveling to Timbuktu, in the West African nation of Mali, is no perilous undertaking, but the city retains the allure of long-forbidden, unattainable places. And with the Niger River as my road, leading me to villages where camels amble and tribesmen with swords stride down the streets, my journey carried the heady whiff of adventure.

I was also able to visit the Dogon, industrious farmers who live in fortresslike villages clustered around the Bandiagara escarpment within the great bend of the Niger. In this rocky stronghold of sacred sites and secret rituals, I stepped into a world that has intrigued Westerners for decades.

From Bamako, Mali's capital, photographer Maggie Steber and I set out by car for Mopti, a town of some 60,000. There we rented a motorized pirogue for the trip down the Niger to Timbuktu—a distance of about 240 miles. Traveling in November, we avoided the summer rainy season and the grueling heat that begins in March and lasts till October. With us was Mamadou Keita, a Malian who spoke flawless French and near-perfect English. Though the voices we heard along the way spoke in various languages—Songhai, Fulfulde, Bozo, Tamachek, Arabic—in almost every village people knew some French, the official language of the country. And Mamadou could always translate into English what I failed to understand in French.

While Mamadou went shopping for last-minute supplies—salt, sugar, and tea for gifts, and bottled drinking water, mosquito netting, kerosene, oranges, and watermelons for us—I wandered through Mopti's lively streets. On the wide avenue along the river, fishermen's wives fried small dogfish to sell, and barbers shaved customers—using their razors on heads rather than chins. Vendors, hugging the walls for shade, crouched beside their trays of hard candies and cigarettes, which were usually sold one at a time.

Traffic was light—leaving ample room for a herdsman driving his sheep and goats to sell them at the marketplace. Other pedestrians had also walked in from the countryside—women with large bundles of firewood balanced on their heads, a girl holding a live chicken by its legs as if it were a flower, and schoolgirls in candy-pink uniforms.

The cobbled quay was a scene of bustling commerce, clogged with crowds and merchandise. Laborers lugged sacks of millet and rice and slabs of rock salt the size of tombstones from big 90-foot cargo pirogues. Ferry pirogues slowly filled with passengers until they were as jammed as city buses.

Carrying baguettes of French bread from the market, I joined Maggie aboard our pirogue, a long, wide canoe with an outboard mounted at the stern and a mat canopy for shade. The crew was ashore buying fuel for our river journey, a transaction that took almost two hours.

Boatman Ahmadou Maiga and his assistant, Alhousseyni Coulibaly, wore turbans twisted into fat coils that swirled around the head and chin. Slits for the eyes were covered by dark sunglasses, so only the men's lips were exposed. Also part of the crew was Ahmidou Traore, a shy 13-year-old with a soft smile whose job was to bail the water that seeped slowly into the center of the boat.

On board, Alhousseyni was earnest and industrious; ashore he wowed the village girls with a Western chic that featured a blue jogging suit, a green scarf draped over a shoulder, and inflatable high-top sneakers unlaced at the ankles. A generation older and graver, Ahmadou had spent most of his working life on pirogues, but his greatest dream was to own a motor-driven pump to draw water from the Niger to irrigate his family's plot of land.

"Then I would become a cultivator like my father and grandfather," Ahmadou told us as we chugged out into the wide, khaki green river that flowed gently northeast toward the desert plains of Timbuktu.

The sight of the glistening Niger meandering across a land that stretches flat and sere to far horizons has been called one of nature's wonders. Even more remarkable is the river's annual flood. Beginning as early as June, the Niger, swollen by summer rains in highlands to the west, slowly spreads over an area twice the size of New Jersey, transforming a section of the semiarid Sahel into one of Africa's great wetlands, known as the Inland Delta. This mosaic of marshes, lakes, and shallow, braided streams that run only after the rains extends from an area south of Mopti northeast to the region around Timbuktu.

Millions of shorebirds and waterfowl, mostly from Europe and Central Asia, winter in the delta, and all that first day on the river we marveled at the graceful succession of herons, egrets, and storks skimming over the water with a lazy flapping of wings. The stilt-legged waders flew low, never ascending into the great, empty vault of the sky. On the banks, clusters of white birds roosting in trees looked like fallen clouds.

While the delta is underwater, the Fulani and Tuareg, the pastoral peoples of the Niger, feed their herds of sheep and goats on grasses that sprout with the summer rains. By November those seasonal pastures have withered, and the nomads move slowly toward the retreating waters, finding forage in harvested fields. By January they arrive at pastures along the Niger, to graze land renewed by the flood.

The migration had begun, and small herds trailing a haze of dust were a common sight on the flat, clay banks. Every few miles we passed a village with the minaret and the crenellated walls of a mosque jutting above the low huddle of flat-roofed houses. Solitary trees—doum palms, figs, or acacias—brought dabs of green to the relentless beige. There were always women at the water's edge—bathing themselves or a child, filling buckets, washing clothes or dishes.

At dusk on the first day we arrived in Koubi, a village of farmers. The chief designated the house of Samba Sangare as the place where we would spend the night. Dozens of children followed us through the door into the small courtyard. Samba tried to shoo them away, but otherwise he was delighted by the parade of visitors our presence brought to his home.

We sat on mats sharing our food with Samba and the men who drifted in. I asked Samba if his wife, sitting away from the group, would like some watermelon. "She doesn't know it and doesn't want it," he replied, with a dismissive wave of the hand.

Seen in the glow of lamplight and the flicker of cooking fires, Koubi reflected almost nothing of the modern world. The sounds of morning—the braying of donkeys, the crowing of roosters, and the call to prayer—began the day at 4 a.m., as they have for centuries. But in the fields the steady rumble of an irrigation pump added a modern note to life in Koubi. So did the blare of rock music from a portable cassette player carried on the shoulders of a young man who had returned from Bamako to help with the harvest.

We continued downriver the next day and joined a small fleet of pirogues full of merchandise and merriment moving in the same direction. All were headed toward the village of Kona, which was holding its weekly market.

"These markets are important village events and not just places to buy and sell," said Mamadou, as Alhousseyni poled the pirogue to shore. "They are a source of news, entertainment, and romance."

The produce spread out on mats in Kona included pink sweet potatoes; black, olive-like fruit called *zegene;* brown karite nuts used to make a butter; red-purple kola nuts, a chewable stimulant of West Africa; and bundles of henna leaves, which women use to darken their palms. Plastic shoes, bead necklaces, soap, combs, zippers, hair pomade, and bags of rice were also for sale. Conversation and banter seemed as important as commerce.

"It's not polite just to go up to a merchant and ask him the price. You should at least begin with a greeting," said Mamadou, stopping in the tailors' section of the market, where men were bent over treadle sewing machines. A herdsman striding along with a spear caught my eye. His coolie hat, broad brimmed and peaked, marked him as a Fulani herder, as did his slender build, fine-chiseled features, and caramel-colored complexion.

Another man pulling a reluctant goat by its ears wore traditional Tuareg garb—a voluminous robe with loose folds, called a *boubou;* a turban draped to cover his mouth; and small leather talisman pouches hanging from a cord around his neck.

A pageant of humanity swirled through Kona: Fulani milkmaids with decorative black stains around their lips; dark-skinned Bella women (whose ancestors were Tuareg slaves) with a fringe of tiny plaits framing their faces; and pale, hawk-nosed Moors, town merchants. These delta people turned drab mud villages and the interminable scrub landscape into a feast for photographer Maggie and into a source of never-ending fascination for me.

Each of the many ethnic groups specializes in an occupation—herding, farming, trading, or fishing. The Bozo are the fishermen. On the river I always saw them in twos—curly-haired, wiry figures in shorts or pants rolled to the knees, poling slender canoes with an effortless, muscular grace. From time to time, the man standing in the prow would swing a large seine net into the water, his profile looming large over the long, flat horizon.

Soon after leaving Kona, we stopped at a Bozo camp. It was a temporary settlement of lean-tos, used only during the fall and winter fishing season. When high water fills the dry watercourses, the Bozo become river nomads, following dense schools of silvery, sardinelike *tineni* that migrate through the flooded delta.

Over small fires at the water's edge, women were smoking the day's catch. Like the millet that comes from the land, the small, oily tineni is a staple in the delta. But the prize fish is the large, sweet-fleshed Nile perch, locally called *capitaine,* which is shipped by fast boat to the Mopti market.

As we were about to push off, an elderly woman approached us, timidly asking for some medicine for a pain in her chest. In almost every village we faced similar requests. Maggie gave the woman some aspirin, while our boatmen carefully explained that the pills would not be a cure.

Ahead of us stretched the broad expanse of Lake Débo, a year-round body of water in the river flats that is sustained by the Niger's flow. "A veritable sea," wrote French traveler Felix Dubois at the turn of the century. "Its shores are invisible, for no distant mountains betray their boundaries. . . ."

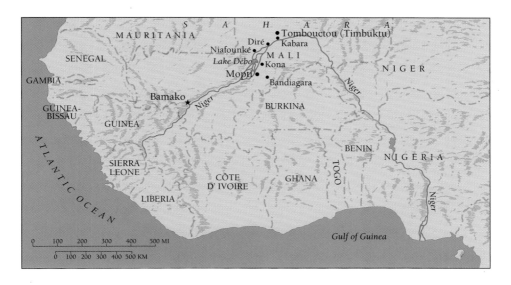

*From Mopti to Timbuktu the Niger waters a thirsty land;
east of the river Dogon villages cling to the Bandiagara escarpment.*

Ahmadou had been worried about wind, which can churn the lake into steep waves, but the day was calm, and the only ripple on the surface was the froth of our wake. Yesterday's hot, dry winds had left a yellow-gray haze that veiled the sun. The water, the color of nickel, merged with a sallow, tarnished sky.

As we moved close to the north shore of the lake, we came upon a luxuriant prairie of *bourgou* abounding with birds. This thick, coarse-bladed grass sprouts in the floodplain and becomes pasture when the waters retreat.

At the far end of the lake, where it drains back into the Niger, we stopped for the night at the bustling village of Youvarou. Because of poor rains, this part of the Sahel was running out of grazing early in the season, and donkey carts piled high with bourgou cut from the marsh trundled through the streets bringing fodder to the herds.

"Come meet the chief and the village elders," said Mamadou as we walked up the broad beach that was the hub of life in the village.

Six men were sitting cross-legged under a canopy of straw mats. One man, off to the side, was mending a fishing net, using his big toe as a peg to hold one end. Elders gathered on the beach every day to discuss village affairs and to socialize. It was a male preserve, where no local women would venture, but out of courtesy to *toubabs*, as foreigners are called, Chief Ibrahim Abdulayi indicated a place where Maggie and I might sit.

A Polaroid camera always gave us a head start in these first encounters. People gathered around to watch figures and faces take shape on the film, and by the time we finished admiring the photographs and making presents of them, a little of the wariness of strangers faded away.

A village chief is responsible for settling local disputes—usually over money or women—but that afternoon more time was spent exchanging greetings with people who came by. These were not simple salutations; they were conversations that inquired about wives, children, and parents as well as in-laws and animals, and that invoked many benedictions. Such litanies can be heard whenever friends or acquaintances meet. The words are chanted mechanically, and sometimes the speakers have walked past each other by the time the dialogue is over, but a simple "how are you?" seemed paltry and cold in comparison.

We left Youvarou the next morning and headed toward the small town of Niafounké. The wind was high, whipping the pale green water into whitecaps. Along the banks of the river the stamp of the desert grew stronger with every hour. Villages with their small areas of green, irrigated fertility were farther apart. The tawny landscape of scrub was baked to sand right down to the river's edge, where egrets stepped daintily in the shallows.

In Niafounké, graceful neem trees and tamarisks lined broad, sandy streets that led from the *Campement,* the government-owned rest house, to one of the schools. I had an appointment with Aly ag Abdou, a schoolteacher who longs for a camel, a well, and a tent so that he might return to the nomadic life in the grand desert spaces. Aly is a Tuareg—tall and lean, with the grave reserve of his people. Like many Tuareg, who have been hit hard by a series of severe droughts and have lost their herds, he has moved to town. But Aly remains a nomad in his heart.

"Many Tuareg have learned new trades in places like Niafounké, but give them five goats, and they will leave for the bush," said Aly, in French. "In the old days there were Tuaregs who never came to town. The head of the family would go there only to buy sugar and tea—the necessities the nomads lacked. Otherwise they lived on milk, cheese, butter, and meat from their herds."

The slight and smiling headmaster of the school, Ali Daou, is also heir to nomadic traditions—those of the Fulani. While the Tuareg were continually on the move with their herds, following the same circuit each year, the Fulani ranged widely for pasture part of the year, but then returned to a village home base when the grasses shriveled.

Ali also has a high regard for old ways. He lives in a traditional compound that includes a corral for livestock; a chicken coop; a narrow loom for his uncle, a weaver; and a Fulani-style domed thatch house where relatives live. He and his family occupy a small adobe structure. Ali's big departure from tradition is his propane-operated refrigerator; by lantern light it looms in the shadows like some oversize white fetish in a pagan temple.

"Personally, I'd rather buy a cow than own a refrigerator," said Ali. "But in my job as headmaster I entertain a lot of official guests, and I need to store a supply of food and cold drinks."

About 200 boys and girls attend this government school. The children learn French early. In fact, the first three years are devoted to teaching the language, and by the fourth grade education is completely in French.

Small Koranic schools, run rather informally by the Muslim clergy, also hold classes. There the students memorize Islam's holy Koran, chanting the Arabic verses at the top of their lungs.

As we left Niafounké, other river travelers, surrounded by their baggage, rimmed the quay waiting for transportation. Maneuvering through the crowd were donkeys carrying sacks of grain from canoes to merchants in town.

On the river, Maggie and I had cherished the hope of seeing hippos. After all, the very name "Mali" means "hippopotamus" in the Bambara language. In 1896 Felix Dubois wrote of seeing the timid beasts "thrust their pink muzzles out of the water. In the solitudes beyond human habitation the timid hippopotamus . . . gambols grotesquely. . . ." Even today it's possible to find hippos, but we were not so lucky. Other animals that once left their tracks—lions, elephants, warthogs, hyenas—have completely disappeared from the riverbanks.

Local people preserve the memory of this wildlife in animal fables told by *griots,* village bards. I heard one such story downriver in Bala Maoundé. As the villagers listened intently and nodded their heads at the familiar lines, Madju Alhousseyni intoned the story of the hyena, the lion, and the ram in a deep, sonorous voice. A highly abridged version goes like this:

Once, a hyena coveted a big pot of honey belonging to a ram. The cowardly hyena, seeking help from a lion, ran off to tell him about this "very good thing" the ram had. Intimidated by the lion, the ram let him taste the honey, while the hyena hovered nearby. "This is very delicious," said the lion. "But," replied the ram, "you don't know how good it really is until you taste the honey flavored with hyena." So the lion ate the hyena, and the ram saved himself and had his revenge at the same time.

We had come to Bala Maoundé to see the phenomenon of floating rice. The crop is sown before the flood begins; it grows with the rising waters, and while the long stems are still half-submerged, farmers harvest the rice in pirogues.

A short walk from the village brought us to the startling sight of navigable fields embraced on three sides by sand dunes. With pretty Nana Diallo Hama, a village agent for CARE, an international aid organization that sponsors such development projects as building dikes, digging wells, and planting trees, I set out across the sea of rice. The tall stalks parted and then closed around the canoe as we glided through jade green vegetation. A tiny red bird, the size of a gumdrop, landed to peck on the ripening grain. Instantly, the whoosh of a slingshot chased the bird away.

"At this time of year, when the rice is almost ripe, the most important task of the village is keeping the birds from devouring the crop," said Nana in fluent French, showing me lumps of clay that were weapons in the war against birds. "Everyone in the village shapes these things, each of us producing about 400 a day. The kids know if they are not out there with their slingshots, they're not going to eat."

Farther downriver I saw other children at work in the village of Koura. They were helping the women irrigate the community vegetable garden by carrying water from the river in pails. A three-year-old was part of the procession, emptying his half-spilled cup on the plants, and, like the others, returning again and again for more water.

"People used to think eating greens was for animals. Now we are glad to eat vegetables," said Chief Ahmadou Amidoun Toure, speaking in Songhai. A regal figure in purple boubou and yellow turban, he had welcomed us with the words, "A stranger among us is like a prince," and then immediately sent for some chairs, insisting we sit on them.

For several years he had worked in the French West African cities of Dakar and Abidjan as a supermarket clerk, airline agent, and merchant. When his father became too old to carry the burdens of a chief, Ahmadou Toure came home. Now that he is back, he finds life in the village "better for the soul." Though the drought was casting a shadow over Koura, adversity had not erased the smiles or stifled the laughter.

"Everything is the will of Allah. We are waiting for the time when Allah shall bless us with more rain," Chief Toure told us.

"*Inshallah*—God willing," we responded, knowing it was the proper reply.

On the last day of our river trip, we left the Niger and turned into a canal, its sluggish waters a lustrous furrow knifing through pale sand flats. Before long, we arrived at the port of Kabara, a small village five miles from Timbuktu. After saying farewell to the crew, we took a taxi to the city that has fired the imagination of so many for so long.

A paved avenue led to the Place de l'Indépendance, where sturdy buildings with crumbling porticos housed government offices. A white statue of a robed warrior on horseback rode in permanent gallop above the dusty greenery of a small, deserted park. The figure represents El Faroukh, the legendary protector of Timbuktu. More modern guardians in military khakis strolled in and out of the army post, where two soldiers and a small cannon stood sentry at the gate.

Only donkeys, pedestrians, and bicycles can move through the narrow streets of the old quarter dominated by the Grand Mosque—Djingereyber—erected in 1336. What the mosque lacks in grandeur, it makes up for in piety, and the muezzin's call from the stubby minaret of mud draws worshipers whose faith has not lost its medieval fervor.

From its beginnings in the 11th century as a seasonal camp for Tuareg, Timbuktu rose to glory in the 14th century as a meeting place for those "who travel by camel or by canoe." The city also became a center of Islamic scholarship, giving rise to the 16th-century adage: "Salt comes from the north, gold from the south, and silver from the country of the white man; but the word of God and the treasures of wisdom are only to be found in Timbuktu."

Timbuktu's decline began in 1591, when Moroccans sacked it, and the city sank deeper as commerce shifted from trans-Saharan trade to shipping along the West African coast. Now the only camel caravans arriving in the city come from the salt mines of Taoudenni, some 400 miles to the north. After a three-week journey, the camels are steered into the city late at night, when it is quiet. If the nervous creatures were to panic and bolt, they might break the 40-pound slabs of salt they carry into less valuable small pieces.

Jiddou ag Ali Moustapha and his band of Tuaregs own several even-tempered camels. Before the French raised their flag over Timbuktu in 1893, and before stern-faced Foreign Legionnaires established a fort in the city, Jiddou might have ridden those camels on raids, plundering caravans or extorting tribute from the residents of the city. Today the camels carry foreigners to his encampment to see a performance of Tuareg dances.

Jiddou approached us with the aloof dignity that characterizes his people. Of a Tuareg's imperious manner, it has been said, "Even when he begs a cigarette, he does so with the air of a king conferring an honor on a subject."

A deal was struck, and at three o'clock one afternoon the camels were kneeling about a hundred yards from our hotel.

Ensconced in wooden saddles, Maggie, Mamadou, and I rocked along into an emptiness of scraggly thorn trees, scraps of grass, and steep sand dunes, lion-colored in the sunlight. Less than two miles away, some 30 Tuareg women, all in indigo robes, waited for us in a wide semicircle, their silhouettes printed on the infinite sky like a frieze on a Grecian urn. Two women played small drums; the rest sang and clapped in unison, swaying with the slow, pulsing rhythm of their music. From time to time one, two, or three men would enter the semicircle, brandishing swords and moving with measured steps.

At intermission, Jiddou served tea in tiny glasses, and we drank the traditional three servings. "The first brew," explained Jiddou in French, "is as strong as death; the second is as hard as life; the third is as sweet as love." Jiddou sometimes spoke of wanting to live as his parents did, before drought destroyed their herds. "But even now, I am still a nomad," he would assert, speaking in the low, impassive voice I had heard many Tuareg use.

As we left for Timbuktu, a winsome young boy jumped up behind my saddle. Tapping me on the back every few minutes, he presented a series of small trinkets for sale. After a while, he nimbly slid down the spine of the camel and sauntered toward home. A small figure in a billowing robe, he added a special grace to the stark landscape.

Like the Tuareg, and the Arab, Songhai, and Bella residents of Timbuktu, the Dogon cultivators of the Bandiagara escarpment about a hundred miles to the south live on the edge of survival. In their language the word "Dogon" also refers to a hardy wild grass that endures despite drought.

East of the Niger in Dogon country, nature is not kind, but it is beautiful. The sandy, impoverished soil yields a millet harvest—if the fickle rains fall, and if swarms of locusts do not devour the crop. The craggy cliffs, honeycombed with caves, soar majestically above the featureless plain, hauntingly beautiful in the glowing colors of sunrise and sunset.

In this sere landscape of luminous rock and massive baobab trees, the Dogon have built fortresslike mud and stone villages like no others on earth. Their granaries, taller and narrower than their houses, are protected from rain by conical caps of straw, often tilted at rakish angles.

Each village has a *togu na*, an open-air house of words. Women are forbidden entry; the men sit under a roof supported by wooden pillars. Many of the pillars were once elegantly carved, but those have been sold and are now on display in museums and art collections around the world.

W hat make the Dogon utterly intriguing are their sophisticated sculpture, dramatic masked dances, and rich spiritual life. While Islam has forged a limited unity among the diverse people along the Niger, most Dogon cling to their animist traditions with remarkable tenacity. Even if they say they are Muslim or Christian, they dance with masks to honor the dead and drink beer and take part in secret burial rites in caves high up in the cliffs.

"When I arrive in a village, I never walk around alone because there are always sacred things I should not touch and sacred places where I should not go," said Stephenie Hollyman, a photographer who was spending six months with the Dogon on a Fulbright Senior Research Fellowship. "Four stones lying on the ground may enclose a holy spot. A small twig with leaves under a rock may be guarding the spirit of someone who has recently died."

Stephenie had invited me to join her and Nouhoum Toumonte, her French-speaking Dogon guide, for a short trip to a few of the villages less frequented by tourists. There are several hundred Dogon communities along the hundred-mile length of the Bandiagara Cliffs— on the plateau above, on the plains below, and nestled against the steep scree slopes at the base of the bluffs themselves.

The town of Bandiagara, the administrative center for the region, is an hour's drive from Mopti on a good dirt road. Stephenie and Nouhoum were waiting with Baba Tembely and his donkey cart when I arrived in Bandiagara, and we jounced for nine miles to the village of Djiguibambo on the edge of the plateau. Nouhoum wore a T-shirt and pants; Stephenie and I wore long, full skirts.

"A woman's exposed knee is rather like a bare buttock," said Stephenie. "I've seen Dogon in an agony of embarrassment as a tourist in shorts sits down beside them, hugging her knees, and tries to make conversation."

At 23, Nouhoum has been a butcher and house-builder and a sought-after guide for the past ten years, helping the Peace Corps and visitors like Stephenie. His advice is always good.

"It is better to ask people about their work, for the Dogon are proud of what they do," Nouhoum said.

His round, friendly face took on a grave look. "If you question them about their beliefs, most of the time you will not get answers, for there are many things about Dogon life that are secret. Even the Dogon boys have to be worthy of learning the ancient lore and the words of Sigi So, the language used in the burial ceremonies in the caves."

A man pedaled by on what locals call an "iron horse," and Nouhoum added, "These days with so many men going off to the city to find jobs, the secrets are in danger of disappearing—like the rains."

Encountering Dogon at work was easy. It was just after the millet harvest, and it was the time for growing onions, the crop of the winter season. All day long people carried yellow calabashes of water to their small, green gardens. Others gathered plants to feed livestock and collected wood for the cooking fires.

Within the village boundaries, the days were sonorous with the sound of women pounding millet. Arms moving up and down like pistons, the women wielded heavy wooden pestles five feet long to crush the husks and pulverize the kernels into flour. Young girls using smaller pestles kept pace with their mothers. There was a rhythm to the way they worked, as there was a cadence to the way the women drew water from the deep wells and the way they walked with large loads on their heads. It was as if they moved in harmony with some music that sounded in the soul.

Throughout the late afternoon we saw a parade of women returning from market day at Bandiagara. In those cooler hours, I decided to leave the donkey cart and jog for a while. One woman joined me on my run, smiling as she kept pace. But there was a difference between us; she was bearing a heavy basket on her head and carrying a baby on her back. And she had walked some 14 miles that day.

Near dusk we arrived in Djiguibambo, where we spent the night. The next morning we hiked a steep, stony trail down the escarpment to the plains and continued along a sandy trail to the village of Téli.

Chief Ali Guindo welcomed us to his compound, where his youngest wife was doing the laundry in a pail, and the older two were pounding millet.

"The last wife is always the best," said Ali, leaving no doubt who his favorite was.

From his roof, where we slept, we could see the abandoned village of old Téli stacked tightly against the cliffs like a scene from a cubist painting. Old Téli had been forsaken in the drought of 1984, but things holy still abide there — the fetishes, stored in clay pots; the sacrificial altar, a mound of earth stained with the blood of chickens; and the oldest member of the community, the *hogon* — or spiritual leader — himself.

Ali accompanied us up the slopes to the cliffs, carrying the chicken we would present to the hogon. We asked permission to enter the small chamber where he sat — a sinewy man with white hair and trim beard, twisting strips of bark from a baobab tree into rope that would be used to hoist the dead into the burial caves high above.

Courtesies were exchanged as we looked out across the broad plain, shimmering in radiant sunlight.

"It's best to let a little time pass before asking the hogon questions. You'll know you've broken the ice if he looks at you and makes eye contact," said Stephenie.

After a while, the hogon raised his head from the rope he was making and looked straight at me with keen, appraising eyes. But there seemed no point in asking a trivial question, and it would have been presumptuous to seek answers of a more meaningful sort.

I stepped outside, savoring those last hours of my journey, remembering the chance pleasures and random surprises that are the essence of any adventure. A young boy sat beside me and began to play a small flute. Its reedy melody drifted through the deserted lanes of old Téli. The boy held my hand, and we walked back down to his home. That simple melody and his sweet, smiling face will always remind me of all the joyful people of the Niger, who temper the harshness of their land with the vitality of their spirit.

Henna designs decorate the hand of a camera-shy woman in Timbuktu. She will peel the tape off when the stain dries. A variety of fashions and customs color life in the ancient city.

FOLLOWING PAGES: Ornate studded door recalls the days when Timbuktu prospered on trans-Saharan trade. By the 17th century, as commerce shifted to the coast, the city's greatness had faded.

*H*is face shrouded to the eyes in Tuareg fashion, Atta ag Mohammed, a member
of the artisan class, displays swords forged for sale to tourists in Timbuktu. Traditionally, these
craftsmen made tools, saddles, and jewelry for their Tuareg patrons, the pastoral nomads
who graze livestock in the arid grasslands just south of the Sahara. As recent droughts devastated
their herds, many Tuaregs moved to towns for jobs. Robed in indigo-dyed cloth,
Atta's daughter-in-law (above) sips tea at home. Women of this caste specialize in leatherwork.

In a city once famed for its piety and scholarship, old and rare books, such as a 16th-century illuminated manuscript (opposite), now find safekeeping in the Ahmed Baba Center of Documentation and Research. Established in 1972, it has collected more than 6,000 volumes from private libraries. On Friday, the Muslim Sabbath, a woman prays in the Djingereyber Mosque, first built in 1336.

FOLLOWING PAGES: Sand dunes at the edge of town provide a playground for Tuareg boys. Many of Timbuktu's 30,000 residents are Songhai, descendants of empire builders who ruled West Africa from 1464 to 1591. Arabs, originally from Morocco, now conduct much of the city's commerce.

Beneath the sparse shade of a low straw-mat canopy, a vendor (opposite) awaits a sale after
pounding slabs of salt into small pieces. An age-old caravan trade survives, still supplying
Timbuktu's marketplace with salt from the Sahara. Motorized river pirogues transport the seasoning
from Timbuktu's port of Kabara, five miles away, to other towns along the Niger. A string
of camels (above), led by Tuaregs, departs Timbuktu for Mali's salt mines in Taoudenni,
some 400 miles to the north. Once, caravans carried gold, ivory, and slaves from the south
to the Mediterranean and returned with fabrics, weapons, sugar, and tea, after stopping en route at
Taoudenni for salt. Camel-mounted, marauding Tuaregs preyed on the Sahara caravans until the
early 1900s, when the French Foreign Legion began patrolling the desert from outposts like Timbuktu.

Music makers clap hands and chant a solemn, haunting Tuareg song to entertain tourists visiting their camp near Timbuktu. The women also set the rhythm for a sword dance the men execute. Such performances earn these victims of drought some income.

*A*rriving in the town of Diré at sunset, "second mate" Alhousseyni Coulibaly stands at the bow, directing his pirogue to a moorage alongside a river ferry. The motorized pirogue carried the author and photographer on a 237-mile voyage down the Niger to Timbuktu. At a Bella encampment of straw-mat huts, housewives (right) wash dishes in the canal leading from the river to Kabara. Annual flooding of the Niger brings life to pastures and fields of rice and millet.

FOLLOWING PAGES: Stubby minaret spires adorn a sunbaked mud mosque in Togonrogo. A Fulani girl rests on the podium where the muezzin stands to call villagers to prayer. Her people, the dairymen of Mali, graze cattle and sell milk throughout the Inland Delta.

*L*ifeline for communities along its banks, the Niger carries most of the commerce of the Inland Delta
in pirogues. A boatman poles a water taxi (opposite) past domed Bella huts on the outskirts of Diré,
a trading center of some 10,000 inhabitants. Few paved roads connect the towns and villages of the
region, but air service links Timbuktu to Bamako, Mali's capital. At sunset, a haze of dust hangs over
the harbor at Youvarou—kicked up by the crowds who had come to the village market on the beach.

FOLLOWING PAGES: Daily chore of threshing millet can serve as a social occasion for women
east of the Niger in Dogon country, a region of several hundred villages along the cliffs of Bandiagara.
Women crush the grain, a mainstay of the Dogon diet, and mix it with water to make a paste.

*N*o women allowed: In the togu na, *the open-sided building where Dogon males gather to rest and discuss village affairs, a man wearing a typical cap and tunic weaves a rope from fibers he unraveled from a nylon sack. Pillars decorated with mythological figures support the thatched roof.*

*R*appeling *down the Bandiagara Cliffs after collecting guano, a Dogon climber (opposite) pauses
above the ledge-top granaries built by the Tellem, the previous inhabitants of the escarpment.
As the Tellem did, the Dogon bury their dead in cliff caves. Irrigating the hard way, a farmer (above)
bears water to his onions in a gourd. Millet, the main crop, depends on summer rains.*

*FOLLOWING PAGES: Straw-hatted granaries store millet, jewelry, and other Dogon valuables.
In her family compound, a housewife wearing the traditional indigo wraparound skirt pours grain
into a basket. A woman's day begins early, when she draws water from a well. She also pounds
millet, gathers firewood, and works beside her husband in the fields. On market days, the high point
of her week, she may walk for miles bearing a heavy load of produce on her head.*

ICELAND

LAND OF FIRE AND ICE

*Volcanoes, earthquakes, and glaciers on this island
at the edge of the Arctic have forged Iceland's stark yet striking
terrain and its resourceful people.*

By Thomas O'Neill   Photographed by Jay Dickman

T
he choice was about as clear as the heavy gray sky that pressed down on us. The lava route or the sand route? Both were crude vehicle tracks that led into the uninhabited interior of Iceland. On the map their dotted traces set out boldly across the empty spaces. Reality was a different story.

The sand route straggled along the northern edge of Vatnajökull, the largest glacier outside of Greenland and Antarctica. Not limited to a valley or a hillside, Vatnajökull sprawls across an entire mountain range. A driver on the sand route can run into quicksand, unbridged glacial rivers, washed-out roadbeds, and blinding fog.

The lava route is no carriage lane either. It winds through a harsh volcanic desert beset by sandstorms and blizzards. Crossing the rough, heaped-up lava fields can take months off your vehicle.

"Take the lava route; it's been so wet the sand route is hard to follow." Our hitchhiker spoke with the confidence of an oracle. Photographer Jay Dickman and I believed him. We had met the hitchhiker—a university student from Germany—at a last-chance gasoline pump on the edge of the interior. He said he had been walking across Iceland on the cheap, but had pulled up lame and needed a ride to the north.

Jay and I were traveling caravan style, each in a bulky four-wheel-drive vehicle in case one of them broke down in no-man's-land. Our goal was to sample Iceland's wilderness, which once we left the coastal roads was not hard to find. An island created by ongoing volcanic eruptions, and then eroded by Arctic winds and mammoth glaciers, Iceland presents a landscape that is predominantly raw and barren. American astronauts were sent here to train because the lifeless, igneous terrain could fill in for the moon. The sparse human population

*Sea-foam laps a nearly trackless beach of black basaltic sand near Iceland's southernmost tip.
More than 200 volcanoes, many of them active, form the backbone of this North Atlantic island nation.*

*PRECEDING PAGES: Arctic terns swirl amid ice blocks begrimed by volcanic grit and ash
during their journey to Jökulsárlón, a tidal lagoon along Iceland's southern coast.*

of 251,000 is confined to the coasts, where the towns can seem as incongruous as the moss that grows on the island's lava fields.

Our two vehicles that day in early August looked underdressed compared to many of the rigs parked at the gas pumps. Antennas sprouted like weeds, connected to emergency gear like cellular phones, broadband radios, and long-range navigational systems. Air-intake pipes protruded from various engines, designed to prevent water from entering the carburetors when the vehicles forded deep rivers. One vehicle sported four pairs of headlights; others squatted like lookout towers atop jumbo mud tires. The only normal car in sight was an abandoned, broken-down station wagon, a cautionary sight for the ill-prepared.

Slysavarnafelag Islands — the National Lifesaving Association of Iceland — recommends much of this equipment, especially the phones and radios that may be used to send distress signals. Help is never terribly far away. Some hundred volunteer rescue teams are on 24-hour alert across the Ohio-size island in case travelers are reported lost or missing, which happens 10 or 15 times a summer. Jay and I now warily eyed our stripped-down rental vehicles, filled with four-dollar-a-gallon gas. After kicking our tires and laying in a few more chocolate bars, we took off.

The lava route at first led across a desolate sand-and-gravel plain. The map showed that we were on the Sprengisandur road, part of a 200-mile wilderness route that runs between the north and south coasts. All the grit and rubble had been left behind by successions of shrinking glaciers, ice having covered the island at least ten times in the past. Here and there stood solitary boulders, called Grettir stones after a character in a medieval Icelandic saga who lifted giant rocks to show off his strength. Several times early on we plowed across glacial streams, crossing the swift, chalk-colored waters wherever ripples indicated a shallow bottom.

Fast, unbridged rivers pose the greatest hazard to backcountry travelers, especially on warm days, when the glaciers shed large volumes of water. Jay and I had heard the stories. One spring, a woman and three children drowned at a Sprengisandur river crossing when their high-tired vehicle tipped over in the strong current. That same spring, a seasoned crew of Icelandic travelers out checking the condition of back-country huts had safely crossed a river in the morning. Returning in the afternoon, not realizing that the river bottom had changed, they took the same path, and their vehicle swamped. Two members of the party froze to death before help could arrive. A year earlier, several Japanese geologists had drowned on the same route we were driving. Capt. Hálfdan Henrýsson, chief of the search-and-rescue coordination center for the Slysavarnafelag Islands group, had preached humility when I spoke with him earlier in the capital city of Reykjavík. "People have strong vehicles and they think they can do anything in them. Well, they can't."

Cold rain was slashing down by the time we turned off Sprengisandur and entered the forbidding lava fields. More than a hundred inches of snow and rain may fall each year in the interior, but with the exception of some ground-hugging, tundra-like flowers and colonies of gray moss, the land is as sterile as the Sahara. Precipitation simply sinks through the porous basaltic rock. Our pace slowed to a crawl. All around us stretched a petrified sea of rock. We lost sight of the track. Clambering up on the ridges of gray and black rock, we searched on foot for the cairns that marked our route. As often as not the so-called road led straight across frozen waves of lava or through obstacle courses of sharp-sided boulders.

Our four-wheel drives lurched and hobbled and strained, going deeper and deeper into the volcanic badlands simply on the faith that our maps showed a road. *"Ach!"* cried the hitchhiker repeatedly, his sore knees knocking together as my vehicle stumbled over another lava pile. He was being tossed about as if he were a prisoner in a runaway stagecoach. Only we weren't going fast: After five hours of grueling progress, we had made less than 50 miles.

During much of that time we had seen not a soul—not the begrimed teams of French and German cyclists we had met elsewhere in the stony interior, or the hardy passenger buses that astonish in the way they barrel along desert tracks, or any of the well-equipped road warriors we had eyed at the pumps. The Icelandic name for this remote region is Ódáðahraun, "lava field of evil deeds." According to old stories, outlaws banished by the Althing, the Icelandic court, sometimes hid here in the world's largest lava field. How anyone could survive in a 2,000-square-mile wasteland where in most places even animals don't tread is puzzling. On the northern edge of Ódáðahraun are ruins of a stone shelter used during the winter of 1774–75 by a sheep stealer named Eyvindur Jónsson. He was so desperate during the frigid days of 24-hour darkness that he used his dead horse for a roof, eating off the carcass until spring light shone through the bones, and he could move on.

We had expected to reach the mountains in which Askja crater lies by nightfall, which in early August just south of the Arctic Circle means eleven o'clock. We were still at least 20 miles, or possibly another half day's travel away, when we wearily pitched our tents on a patch of volcanic ash. Through a nearby veil of rain the distant spine of Vatnajökull gleamed white in the last rays of daylight. We shivered.

Fortunately the lava fields soon gave way to a plain of soot gray ash, which we raced across with abandon, our vehicles kicking up tall plumes of dust. The ash desert appeared in the wake of a cataclysmic eruption at Askja in 1875. The fallout blanketed the entire eastern rim of the island, ruining farmlands and triggering a large-scale emigration to North America. A more recent eruption, in 1961, spilled a thick, coal black band of lava across the plain. We now drove slowly past the so-called "stone flood," its liquid origins betrayed by the wavelike sheets of rock that had hardened in mid-flow.

Disembarking near a campground, we hiked through an opening in the mountains and found ourselves in an immense natural amphitheater. Five miles long and four miles wide, this walled-in bowl was formed when an enormous magma chamber here emptied during an eruption, causing the ground to cave in. In 1965 Apollo 11 astronauts came to the Askja caldera to see what the moon might look like. Jay and I set off across the void. On the other side of it we reached Víti—"hell." That's the name given to the explosion crater that in 1875 spewed tremendous amounts of mud and ash into the air. Hell seemed small—a steep-sided, 50-foot-deep hole. It also seemed alive. At the bottom lay a steaming pond of milky blue water warmed by magma in the earth's crust. The air stank of sulfur. Below us we could see tourists skinny-dipping in the crater. Hell was just an exotic Jacuzzi to them.

An even more dramatic relic of the 1875 eruption lay a few steps away. It was Öskjuvatn, a large cold-water lake that sat in the wrinkled landscape like a glass eye. The deepest lake in Iceland at 712 feet, Öskjuvatn was created when the ground suddenly sank after the 1875 eruption, leaving a cavity almost two miles in diameter. Rainwater has filled it up. A group of people merrily picnicking on the lake's barren shore looked as out of place as flowers growing in asphalt.

It is an irony of nature that few things seem colder than a cinder whose fire has just been extinguished. Askja's volcanic wilderness exudes such a terminal chill. Yet so dramatic and alien does this landscape born of fire appear that it beckons like a mysterious ruin. As we hiked back to our vehicles, I had an uncontrollable desire to find the source of the stone flood and to convince myself of the fiery, violent forces that underlie this inert, dungeon-cold place. Leaving the trail, I climbed over the dark ropes of lava, scraping my knees and cutting my hands as I went. Scoria—rough lava fragments that had been tossed into the air like froth—began to appear. Soon I reached a small crater filled with loose, slaglike rocks. Sliding down the side, I came to rest at the center, the dead, plugged-up vent that had once spewed molten rocks from an inferno beneath my feet. Never had the world seemed so foreign.

Iceland, this fiery island in a cold sea, has from its earliest sightings inspired other-worldly visions. A seafaring Irish monk, St. Brendan, is believed by some scholars to have discovered Iceland, because he appears to have witnessed a volcanic eruption in the North Atlantic during one of his voyages in the sixth century. "There came into view a large and high mountain in the ocean . . . ," begins a passage in *Navigatio Sancti Brendani Abbatis,* a sometimes hallucinatory account of Brendan's trip in a leather boat with 17 other monks. The account continues: "Then they saw the peak of the mountain unclouded and shooting up flames into the sky . . . so that the mountain was a burning pyre."

Later, seeing hot rocks being hurled up from the sea, apparently by an underwater explosion, St. Brendan cried out, "Soldiers of Christ, be strong in faith . . . for we are now on the confines of Hell." Irish monks eventually became the first people to settle on Iceland, living in caves on the southern coast during the ninth century. Pagan Vikings from Norway displaced them, first arriving in 874.

Superstitious Christians in the Middle Ages echoed Brendan with their notion that the entrance to hell could be found on Hekla, the oft-erupting 4,892-foot volcano visible to sailors approaching Iceland. The fevered imaginings about what lay beneath Iceland took their most imaginative form in Jules Verne's *Journey to the Center of the Earth.* Verne, a Frenchman who had never been to Iceland but who had avidly read travel accounts of the island, described in his 1864 science fiction novel how Professor Lidenbrock, a German geologist, and his nephew Axel believed that they could reach the center of the earth by climbing down inside the crater of Snæfellsjökull, a dormant, ice-capped volcano that rises boldly from a peninsula on Iceland's west coast. Descending into that mountain, the adventurers discover not fire and brimstone, but a labyrinth of caves filled with prehistoric fossils and a vast inland sea lit by electrical storms. An eruption expels the men from a volcano in Italy.

Fact, however, can be as improbable as fiction in dealing with Iceland's geology. On an island where nearly every mountain is volcanic, so intense and powerful is the subterranean heat that many eruptions have occurred beneath glaciers. Only when the ice sheets retreated were many dark, volcanic heights revealed.

Before I had ventured into the interior, whose few roads and tracks are passable only during the snow-free summer months, I had needed a geology lesson, some way to make Iceland's brooding, bare-knuckled appearance comprehensible. Why is this remote northerly island so volatile? What explains the fact that more than 200 volcanoes have erupted here since the island rose from the sea in a lengthy explosion 26 million years ago? The lesson took place on lava-strewn Reykjanes, a peninsula an hour's drive from the capital city of Reykjavík on the far southwestern coast. The near-shore waters and many of the sea cliffs were mobbed with noisy seabirds—northern fulmars, kittiwakes, and puffins. By contrast the land was deserted. In places it looked as if it had been cauterized with a branding iron. Steam rose from blackened fissures and from scablike ground patches yellowed with sulfur encrustations. Mud puddles boiled. Thick beds of ancient gray-black lava showed ripples and swells as if the molten discharge had only just halted.

"What you're looking at is oceanic bottom," said my teacher, Dr. Páll Imsland, then a volcanologist at the University of Iceland. Like the accomplished lecturer he is, this tall, craggy man in his forties waited for my disbelieving expression before proceeding. Iceland, Páll said, is a rare place where the Mid-Atlantic Ridge— a seafloor mountain range—emerges from the water. These submarine peaks define where two of the gigantic plates that make up the earth's crust—the North American plate and the Eurasian plate—are steadily pulling apart and opening an avenue to tremendous pent-up heat in a layer of hot rock called the mantle. Magma—molten rock—seeps through the rift into the cold ocean depths, where it quickly hardens into

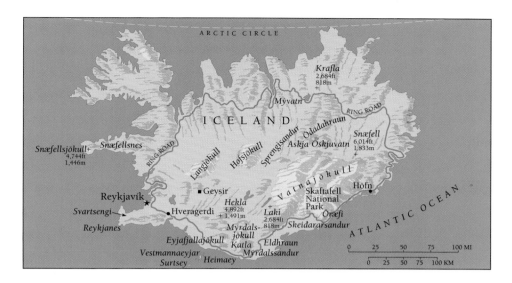

Risen from the depths of the sea, Iceland has been shaped by fire and ice.

basaltic rock. By filling in the spreading fissure between the plates, the rock becomes new ocean floor. In some places on the ridge, oozing magma has built up into underwater peaks more than 12,000 feet high.

The ocean floor rears out of the water at this precise place in the North Atlantic because beneath the island lies a hot spot, a fixed plume of intense heat originating deep within the mantle. Enormous amounts of lava have piled up at the hot spot, more than can be dispersed by the spreading of the seafloor. The result is that a still-growing island—Iceland—has emerged from the waves. "Here at your feet, right now," Páll concluded, "Iceland is being produced."

And Iceland continues to be born, a volcanic manifestation that covers almost 40,000 square miles. The most active volcanic region in the world, Iceland has experienced from the time of the Viking settlement an eruption every five years, on average. Molten rock and tephra—ash, pumice, and other volcanic debris—have burst forth from miles-long fissures, from mountaintop craters, from vents beneath glaciers. The constant seafloor rifting and the resultant upwelling of magma enlarges the geologically young island about three-quarters of an inch a year, a fact that prompted one droll Icelander to say to a visiting journalist, "You'd better watch out for the future. Eventually, we are going to take over."

As I absorbed this information, my thoughts turned downward, below the smoldering, sulfurous ground of Reykjanes we were standing on, all the way to the inner recesses of the earth. Jules Verne was right: Iceland does evoke the center of the earth. The building blocks of the earth's foundation are being manufactured in open view. Here the molten soup beneath the crust feels extremely close. Indeed, in a so-called high-temperature region like Reykjanes—"smoky peninsula"—the readings a thousand feet below us in the lava reach a hellish 600°F.

Any traveler to Iceland who has inhaled the acrid scent of brimstone and has seen the vast cinder fields can thus be forgiven a small spasm of anxiety and excitement and the question it leads to: "Any chance of an eruption soon?"

"It's been a relatively quiet period," said Páll as he peered on tiptoe into a small, fire-blackened explosion crater from the 1300s. "The last eruption was in 1984 in the Krafla area on the northern part of the island, near a lake called Mývatn.

"It was a fissure eruption," he continued, "the most common type of volcanic event in Iceland. You're probably more familiar with cone eruptions, like those in the Caribbean. In a fissure eruption the lava comes out of large cracks that have opened in the ground. No one was evacuated, but some of us worry that the eruptions are coming too close to a geothermal power plant built nearby."

Despite the recent volcanic lull, some of Iceland's most spectacular eruptions have occurred within the last 35 years. On November 14, 1963, a series of tremendous submarine explosions off Iceland's southern coast sent columns of ash and steam more than two miles high. Two days later an island appeared in the roiling water. It was soon christened Surtsey after the Norse fire giant, Surtur. Volcanic activity lasted for the next four years, leaving a still-warm island that covers one square mile.

Ten years later on neighboring Heimaey, in the island group called Vestmannaeyjar, another powerful eruption captured world headlines as a mile-long fissure cracked open, pouring forth lava that would bury a quarter of the island's dwellings. The rest of the homes and one of Iceland's most important fishing harbors were saved when seawater sprayed from high-pressure hoses was used to cool the lava and halt its deadly advance. An orderly evacuation of the town's 5,000 residents prevented any loss of life. American journalist John McPhee later calculated that the amount of lava released in the Heimaey eruption would have been "enough to envelop New York's entire financial district, with only the tops of the World Trade Center sticking out like ski huts." After five months of lava flows, Heimaey had grown by one-third of its former size.

The Krafla fissures in the north of Iceland erupted almost yearly between 1975 and 1984, the fiery events usually preceded by powerful earthquakes. Iceland's most famous volcano, Hekla, which has exploded at least 13 times since the Vikings arrived in the ninth century, returned to life most recently in 1991. In 1970 it had staged what was called the "tourist eruption." Visitors and locals alike safely drove to the foot of the mountain and watched the lava fountain out as if the scene were playing on a drive-in movie screen. The aftereffects were anything but entertaining, however; the ash that fell was so rich in toxic fluorine that 7,000 sheep died in the vicinity.

"Never trust a volcano," Páll told me that day on the Reykjanes peninsula. "In an oceanic rift zone, volcanoes are less defined than on a continental landmass. Fissure eruptions can occur any place within a large area." He sketched on my map the active volcanic zone. It is a broad, discontinuous swath, one arm of which begins on Reykjanes and follows a northeasterly slant—the orientation of the seafloor rift. The other arm leads north from Surtsey and passes east of Hekla. The twin paths meet in the island's center and sweep northward past Askja and Krafla and back into the ocean. Altogether the active zone takes up a third of the island, almost all of it uninhabitable wilderness.

To drive anywhere in Iceland, even into the interior badlands, means spending some time on the coastal Ring Road, a narrow, low-speed highway that, in girdling the island, covers 950 miles. With Páll joining us as commentator, photographer Jay Dickman and I followed the Ring Road, or Highway 1, for several days as we explored the southeast coast, a temperamental realm of glaciers and hot springs, deserts and waterfalls. After the dark, blasted landscape of Reykjanes, I was distrustful of the Irish-green pastureland we encountered as we headed east from the capital. It was as if the landscape had been color-enhanced. Sheep, cows, and horses, their coats growing thick and shaggy in the wet coastal climate, grazed in fields that had taken hold on ancient lava beds. Farmhouses were scattered about, modest white-painted buildings of corrugated iron with red roofs. Occasionally a plain, steepled church graced a farmstead, a reminder of the days when bishops tended the land as well as the soul. The farther east we went, the more forlorn and vulnerable the farms appeared, huddled at the bottom of lava cliffs streaked with waterfalls, or hunched in the shadow of ash-stained glaciers. The farms have staying power, though; many have names extending back to the sagas of the 12th and 13th centuries.

We stopped briefly in the quiet town of Hveragerði, "garden of hot springs," which sits on the edge of the volcanic zone. The energy underground here has been tapped to heat a complex of greenhouses where, as we saw by pressing our faces against steamy panes, a large proportion of the country's tomatoes, cucumbers, and bell peppers are grown. Proud of his land's thermal properties, Páll insisted that the three of us swim a few laps in the naturally heated outdoor community pool. Never before had I swum comfortably in a cold drizzle.

One day we left the Ring Road to see the namesake of all geysers, Geysir itself. Its towering plume of hot water was first noted in the 13th century after a swarm of earthquakes. Unfortunately, Geysir (rhymes with laser) has been moribund this century, perked to life only when powdered soap is poured down its throat. We were left to marvel at the geyser's wide, sinter-encrusted basin, the cannon barrel of its once-formidable 200-foot gush (about 20 feet higher than Old Faithful's). "I predict," said Páll, "that the next big quake will awaken Geysir."

Twenty yards away, a geyser called Strokkur—"butter churn"—has taken over Geysir's mantle, flinging hot water and steam some 50 feet high several times an hour. In relaxed Icelandic fashion no fences seal off Strokkur; people perch on the very rim of the explosive hot spring until a large dome of water suddenly rises from the depths, giving spectators a few seconds in which to dash away before a jet of superheated water fountains into the air.

Returning to the Ring Road, we soon left behind the world of bright colors and entered a stark black-and-white realm. Huge plateau glaciers sprawled over the coastal highlands, fed by the more than a hundred inches of precipitation that fall in the south each year. Tongues of ice crawled down off the heights, their tips warped and wrinkled by crevasses. Between the retreating glaciers and the sea stood lifeless outwash plains of mud and ash. Cool eddies of air swept down from the ice as we drove a primitive single-lane road of cinder and sand. Clouds muffled the icy heights, while below, rain drummed impatiently on the roofs of our vehicles.

As we passed beneath Eyjafjallajökull—"island mountain glacier"—a ridge of snow and ice 5,466 feet high, Páll entertained us with believe-it-or-not tales. Thirty years ago, he said, a small airplane disappeared without a trace above the glacier. Recently the plane reappeared on the lower end of Eyjafjallajökull, having crept down with the ice. The volcanologist next turned to the bleak sands on our right and reported that in the Middle Ages people attributed the desolation here to a battle over boundary rights between two settlers. Possessed of witching powers, the rivals threw rivers onto each other's land, washing away all signs of life.

The 20th-century explanation goes by the name of *jökulhlaup,* or glacial outburst flood, an event unique to Iceland. In a marriage of fire and ice, active volcanoes lie buried under the three large glaciers on the southern coast. When one of these hidden volcanoes erupts, heat melts the overlying ice, releasing tons of water from underneath the glacier, the torrent destroying everything in its path. The most destructive jökulhlaup occurred in 1362, when a flash flood from beneath one of the arms of Vatnajökull to the east obliterated an entire farming community, killing 400 people. That area today is known as Öræfi, "wasteland."

So great is the stored-up power of a jökulhlaup that the water released from the glacier Mýrdalsjökull has in the past exceeded the flow of the Amazon River, the most voluminous watercourse in the world. The glacier's ice-entombed crater, Katla—"kettle"—is historically one of the most active volcanoes on the island, though its last eruption came in 1918. Crossing Mýrdalssandur—"sands of Mýrdal"—we saw nothing but loose gravel and sand, sometimes heaped up in ragged dunes. Dust storms can rage in this cold desert, and we hurried on without stopping.

Then came a vision of green. Brilliant emerald moss stretched in all directions. Jay and I jumped from the vehicle and, like rescued castaways, plunged into the welcoming growth. The rain-washed moss was so soft we let ourselves fall backward into its pillowy embrace. A sea of green rolled and swelled, following the contours of boulders and rocks. That such a plush and gentle terrain could have a violent and tragic story behind it seemed unfair. Beneath the mossy carpet, however, lay lava produced by the largest lava flow eruption in earth's history, an event that unleashed a calamitous period in Iceland's history.

On June 8, 1783, in barren lands to the north, an enormous fissure opened. The crack extended for 15 miles and was studded with more than 100 exploding craters. The molten rock from the so-called Laki eruption flowed for eight months, drowning a 218-square-mile area—twice the size of Chicago—with lava three stories deep. Accompanying the molten flood were towering clouds of poisonous gas that shrouded the island in a lethal blue haze. Some 10,000 people, a fifth of the population, died from famine as crops failed and most of the island's livestock perished.

Now, two centuries later, moss has swallowed up Eldhraun, "field of fire." Hearing Páll relate the awful story stirred in me the same weird sense of dislocation that I had felt at Askja in the interior. I was surrounded by such evidence of natural violence and yet the cause of it—the fires beneath the surface—seemed so alien to the imagination. While traveling in Iceland, I was often overtaken by a sense of brooding uneasiness, as if I were walking a battlefield from a forgotten war.

Continuing our eastward journey, Páll, Jay, and I entered the restless precincts of Vatnajökull. The immense "water glacier" was creating its own weather high above us, trapping clouds that unloaded dark torrents of rain onto the heights. Meltwater poured from its many fingers of ice. The swift glacial rivers, upon reaching the sands of the outwash plain, fragmented into numerous unruly streams. For years flash floods and suddenly changing river courses defied the efforts of engineers to bridge the treacherous Skeiðarársandur, "sands of the river," which fanned out below Vatnajökull. Not until 1974 did a network of roads and bridges finally cross the 18-mile-long desert and thus complete the Ring Road.

An oasis of sorts exists toward the eastern end of the Skeiðarársandur. It is a grove of native trees—birch, willow, and mountain ash. When the Vikings and their Irish slaves arrived, Iceland was much greener, its coastal areas rich in grasslands and woods. But a deteriorating climate and a thousand years of grazing and soil erosion have denuded the countryside. Woodlands once covered perhaps 25 percent of Iceland's surface; today they account for barely one percent of the total.

The singular forest at the foot of Vatnajökull stands at the center of Skaftafell National Park. On a chilly midsummer evening, with the sounds of singing and guitar playing drifting from a nearby campground, I spoke with park warden Stefán Benediktsson, an architect and former member of parliament whose family has farmed in this region since the 1400s. "This site was chosen as our country's first national park in 1967 because of a combination of contrasts in a very small area," the white-haired warden said in English. "You have a huge desert in front, sumptuous growth here at the campsite, and glaciers behind. And we have kept it primitive; no motorized vehicles or horses are allowed in the park."

The warden and I talked briefly about Iceland's tumultuous history of jökulhlaups, fissure eruptions, and earthquakes. Finally I asked if all this violence and unpredictability didn't weigh heavily on the psyches of his fellow citizens. Benediktsson smiled and shook his head. "There's no anxiety factor in Iceland. People here have greater respect for natural forces than for human abilities. You just accept the dangers. Icelanders are survivalists above all."

The humbling force of nature is inescapable when you drive for 150 miles and the same glacier continues to loom outside your window. During that time I could barely take my eyes off the ice-shrouded horizon of Vatnajökull; it filled the mind like a lion's footprint at an African water hole. Captured by the glacier's omnipresent spell, we decided one sunlit night to explore the giant ice cap by snowmobile. We drove up a mountain road to a tentacle of ice called Skálafellsjökull, near the town of Höfn, and, as the moon rose opposite the sun, we roared off over the smooth snow in our rented machines. Soon we were surrounded by an oceanic emptiness. Far in the distance mountain peaks jutted out of the ice like sinister palaces.

Vatnajökull, at 3,240 square miles, lays claim to a twelfth of Iceland's land area. Beneath its frozen surface stirs one of the country's most active volcanoes, Grímsvötn. Its heat has created a huge subglacial lake that periodically overflows to destructive effect. Usually its volcanic activity takes place in secret; during its eruption in 1983, however, Grímsvötn revealed itself with a cloud of smoke and ash that climbed high above the ice.

There was no way to take the measure of this glacial vastness in a few hours. We contented ourselves with driving fast along relatively straight paths, something we could rarely accomplish on the roads below. Before we left the frozen heights of Iceland, I stopped my snowmobile and looked out at the silvery, moonlit Atlantic Ocean. The lights of fishing trawlers traced its surface. I stared at the water for a few minutes. It was reassuring just then to see that something existed other than rock and ice.

Horseshoes had been found on Vatnajökull. Páll told us that they had probably been left behind by farmers, who in past centuries traveled with horses across the high glacier to collect an edible moss from the slopes of the dormant volcano Snæfell. I wasn't surprised. Few places on the rugged island are out of bounds when you can rely on the famous Icelandic horse. Brought to Iceland by early Viking settlers and since then unmixed with any other breed, the small, powerful Icelandic horse has served as a work animal. Today, though they are occasionally used to round up sheep on the mountainsides, these long-maned mounts are best loved as weekend riding horses. Still, nothing suits them better than to plunge into the wilderness.

With the help of Páll and Ingimar Bjarnason, a farmer and noted horse breeder, I arranged a three-day horse trek into remote highlands on the eastern edge of Vatnajökull. To accomplish this journey through demanding country, we required twenty-two horses—two horses apiece for the seven travelers we had assembled, and another eight for carrying gear. The horses made a fine sight the morning we departed. With their manes flying like scarves, legs lifting in a feverish trot, the twenty-two horses set off across the countryside with the eagerness of a cavalry charge, pounding down a river valley toward a wall of mountains.

One of the highest compliments that can be paid an Icelandic horse is that it is "willing." The gray veteran I rode certainly was, tearing off at a manic gallop, almost bucking me when I hauled on the reins. Ingimar rode up to scold me for screaming "Whoa!" "Ingimar says don't yell at the horses," Páll dryly translated. "They don't like to be yelled at."

Single file our cavalcade rode along a ridge above a cloudy, many-armed glacial river called Jökulsá í Lóni. The horses needed little encouragement to wade into a fast-flowing tributary, the frigid water rising to their flanks. The Icelandic horse, which averages only about 14 hands—4½ feet—in height, possesses the unerring step of a mountain goat. One 19th-century admirer described his horse as "sure-footed enough to walk downstairs backwards." That quality was apparent throughout the bright, surprisingly warm day as we rode up and down bare-rock mountains. Sometimes a steep descent would prove too much, and we had to dismount and walk, leaving rockslides in our wake.

Páll was feeling his oats. Crossing the caldera of an ancient volcano, an area of sharp rocks and thin grass, the volcanologist exclaimed, "These are my colors—greens, browns, and grays." He heard me snicker. "I don't like trees," he insisted. "You can't see anything. The desert is the finest landscape."

Occasionally we stopped to rest the horses. While they licked the salt off one another's necks, we ate a snack of *skyr*, a mixture of sweet and sour cream; and *hardfiskur*, dried codfish slathered with butter. The young, redheaded cook, Sigyn Eiríksdóttir, a student of Páll's, apologized for not finding the Americans any *hákarl*, spoiled shark meat, an Eastertime delicacy in Iceland.

By late afternoon our progress became slow and grueling. The horses had a hard time making their way through a dense patch of scrub birch and willow on a lower slope. Several times a welter of branches snagged a packhorse and flipped it onto its back. When we had gained the top of one of the mountains, I fell behind and in the twilight lost the track. I allowed my horse to wander into a patch of wet sand and gravel, and, before I could react, the animal had sunk to its haunches in quicksand. Instinctively the horse reared, tossing me onto the gluey ground. The horse pulled itself out of the morass. Fortunately two of our group came back to look for me. It took a rope to pull me out.

Bone-weary, we pitched camp at midnight in a narrow valley near the ruins of a stone farmhouse. No one had lived in this mountain enclave for at least a century, Páll said. Before that, the valley had served as a hideaway for people accused of crimes of passion. An orphaned brother and sister who had committed incest escaped here with the help of a priest in the 1700s and lived in solitude until their deaths. In the mid-1800s, an outlaw named Stefán Olafsson dropped out of sight here for three years. In modern times, Ingimar Bjarnason with his horses is one of few people to have passed through these lonely hills.

The next day we continued deeper into the hinterlands. On a high, windy ridge we came within sight of a small glacier that fitted the mountaintop like a toupee. A pair of antlered reindeer bounded down a grassy slope. At midday, as a strong wind shook even the horses, we climbed a knoll and saw below us an exquisite steep-walled valley, its river dropping down in a series of waterfalls. After a painstaking descent to the valley floor, all twenty-two horses broke into a gallop, running like quicksilver across a gravelly floodplain. I loosened my reins and held on to the mane. For a brief time my mount dropped into the smooth, swift gait called *tölt*, in which the horse runs like a reindeer, lifting first its right legs, and then its left legs. Despite Ingimar's instructions, I had to holler.

When the hard, invigorating ride had ended, Ingimar gathered all of us inside a cabin and with great solemnity pronounced thanks—thanks to the horses, to his helpers, to the paying guests, and finally to the Lord for allowing the two Americans, slightly green in the horn, to return in one piece. Then he hugged us and kissed our cheeks. I thought of St. Brendan then, and his description of Iceland as hell's gate, and I realized that where there is a hell there is a heaven.

Gray-and-white walls crumble as a glacier recedes from a steam field in the Hveradalir district of central Iceland; meltwater forms a braided river. Glaciers cap a tenth of the island.

FOLLOWING PAGES. Streaked with dirt and debris, Heinabergsjökull fans into a meltwater lake. Streaks form when glaciers converge, heaping rubble into a common ridge called a medial moraine.

*O*n the edge of disaster: The author (left) and traveling companions attempt to retrieve
a snowmobile trapped while trying to negotiate a crevasse on Skálafellsjökull. "Our guide was crossing
a snowbridge when his machine slid off and wedged itself into the chasm," O'Neill said.

*F*leet-footed visitor leaps to the lip of Strokkur—"butter churn"—a geyser near Reykjavík, for a look into its gaping crater. Water welling up within the geyser's throat will signal an impending eruption, an event that takes place several times an hour. Nearby Geysir (opposite), the namesake of all such spouting springs, hurls a plume of superheated steam and water more than 130 feet into the air. Groundwater heated by molten rock provides Iceland with some 800 geysers and boiling springs. Geothermal wells generate electricity and supply hot water to heat many Icelandic homes.

*B*athers relax in the briny waters of the Blue Lagoon, silica-laden runoff from a geothermal plant at Svartsengi. Superheated steam, tapped from as deep as a mile below the surface, spins turbine blades to produce electric power and to heat water that is piped to seven nearby towns. At top output, a comparable oil-fired plant would burn up to 2,400 barrels of oil a day. Pale blue focus in a field of steam (below), a thermal pool beckons in a remote area known as Hveravellir—"plain of hot springs." But bathers beware! This water is scalding hot.

FOLLOWING PAGES: Church and farmhouse keep company beneath the basaltic brow of a ridge on Snæfellsnes, a peninsula that formed the setting for Jules Verne's novel, Journey to the Center of the Earth. Such a scene recalls a time when, according to Verne, the island's clerics were paid "a ridiculously small pittance" that often required them to farm for a living.

*M*oss campion lends a cushion of color to the stark slopes of a crater in the Eldhraun region.
In Iceland's cool climate it may take a century or more for moss to soften a raw volcanic landscape.
A braided river (opposite) threads past a crater formed when a lava flood spilled from
a 15-mile-long fissure across southern Iceland in 1783. The event created scores of craters
and buried an area twice the size of Chicago with lava three stories deep.

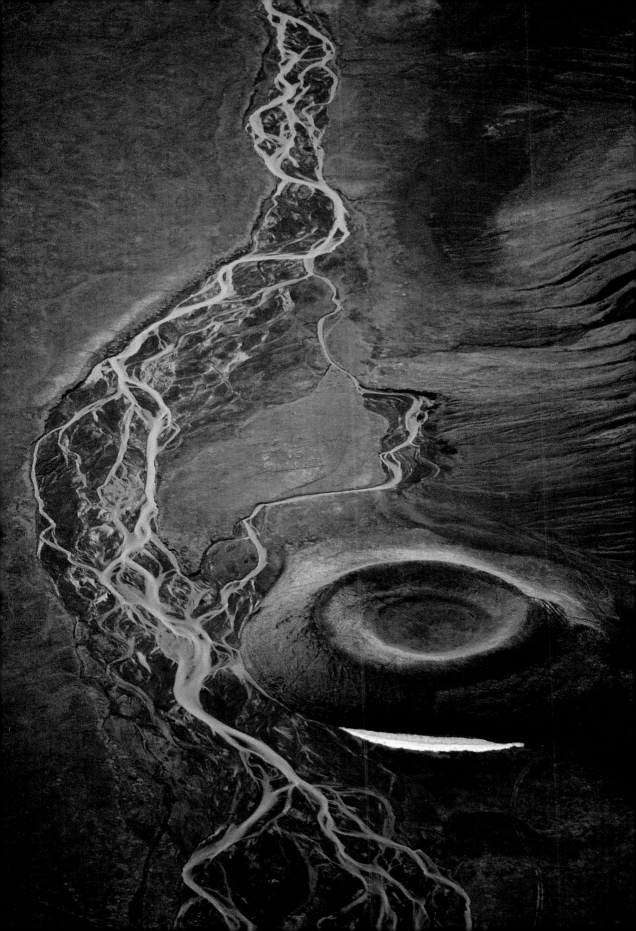

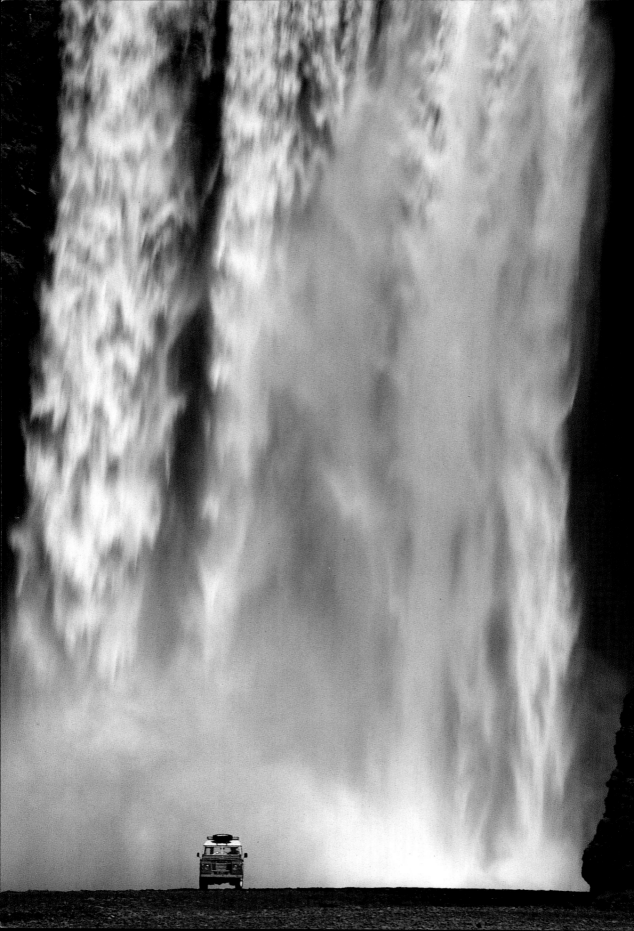

Thundering wall of water, Skógafoss tumbles 197 feet near the highway along Iceland's southern coast. Drivers often park in its mist, using the cascade as a cheap and handy car wash. Sluicing through a moss-covered plain, the Ófæra River in southern Iceland ducks beneath an arch of basalt as it steps into a thousand-year-old volcanic chasm.

FOLLOWING PAGES: Morning mist rises as a farmer rounds up Icelandic ponies in preparation for an excursion into the hinterlands of eastern Iceland. The diminutive horses, descended from Viking mounts, exhibit exceptional stamina, surefootedness, and vitality.

BOB KRIST (OPPOSITE)

*E*veryone walks the hairpin turns and steep scree slopes of Illikambur Canyon on the eastern edge of Vatnajökull. The author's party included (from left) Ingimar Bjarnason, leader of the expedition, and trail hands Halldór Gudmundsson and Jón Einarsson. Crossing a swift-flowing glacial stream during the three-day trek, Einarsson's mount slips and scrambles to keep its footing while the rider lunges across the saddle to maintain balance. He hung on and remounted.

FOLLOWING PAGES: Tall in the saddle, farmer and horse breeder Ingimar Bjarnason moves his Icelandic ponies to saddle them for a trek. The small yet spirited steeds trace their ancestry to Norse mythology and are far more reliable than machines in a land where roads are few and far between.

VENEZUELA

LOST WORLD
OF THE TEPUIS

Ancient, rain-forested mesas shape this mysterious niche of nature—so isolated and so rich in unique species that visitors once thought it the vestige of an earlier Earth, frozen in time.

By Tom Melham Photographed by Jay Dickman

The day begins like a Spielberg movie: We're thundering along in a small helicopter, skimming leafy humps of rain forest canopy as the pilot traces a tannin-stained river upstream, toward its source. Below, two dugout canoes and a few Indian huts provide a bit of human counterpoint to boundless nature. Hills appear, then give way to a gigantic platform looming up like the ruins of a colossal and long-abandoned walled city. It stands about a mile high, absolutely flat topped and sheer sided, rimmed by wandering palisades that resemble deeply folded drapery. Everywhere along its fluted cliffs, waterfalls plummet, creating the illusion of a hundred Yosemites spliced into one immense, meandering wall.

Inside the helicopter, photographer Jay Dickman and I are going through rolls of film like popcorn at a first-run movie. Some members of Terramar—a group of Venezuelan scientists and amateur naturalists devoted to exploring and studying remote areas of their country—are pointing and exclaiming at various features below. Terramar organized this trip, part of a two-week-long swing through southeastern Venezuela.

Sunlight warms the pinkish stone before us to incandescence, revealing profiles that at first seem too carefully sculptured to be from nature's hand. Yet they are too huge *not* to be: The platform's summit rambles free-form over 250 square miles; its walls plunge vertically thousands of feet before ending in squat, buttress-like talus slopes blanketed by rain forest. No, no humans built this citadel, nor have any lived here—ever. Few have even visited it. This is Auyan-tepui—"devil mountain" in local Indian dialect—one of more than a hundred similarly truncated *tepuís,* or table mountains, flung across a 500-mile-long rise of land that forms the southern watershed of the Orinoco River, dividing it from the Amazon. Most tepuis stud

Dagger leaves of Orectanthe sceptrum—*a type of herb—crowd a soggy niche atop Cuquenan, one of Venezuela's ancient and fabled* tepuis—*flat-topped and slab-sided sandstone mountains.*

PRECEDING PAGES: *Head in the clouds, waterfall-spouting Roraima rises 9,094 feet. High rainfall, relatively harsh climate, and limited nutrients make tepui country a repository of unique species.*

Venezuela, though a few occupy border areas of Guyana, Brazil, and Colombia. They are old, scattered remnants of a once vast area of sandstone plateaus, laid down more than a billion years ago, uplifted, then eroded for eons into these massive stumps of stone. Geologists call this area the Guayana shield. Imagine Utah's red-rock country gone bush—its largest and steepest mesas ballooned in size 10- or 20-fold, transplanted from the arid Four Corners to the wet tropics, their stark edges fringed in greenery and frothy with waterfalls—and you have the tepui region of southeastern Venezuela.

It is an otherworldly place: Great slab islands rise from a sea of rain forest and savanna. Their flat summits seem smooth, but up close convulse into rutted and cross-rutted badlands of stone forests and labyrinths, lacy filigrees and gravity-defying stacks. Lagoons, shallow bogs, and yawning sinkholes punctuate them, and rivers wander out from the rubble of collapsed cliffs, only to drop mysteriously from sight. Fields of strange-looking plants grow—thrive even—on "soils" that contain very few nutrients, while animals remain few and all but invisible. Man is a relative newcomer here, having climbed his first tepui just over a century ago; some peaks still await their first human visitor.

E ven now tepui country stands as one of the last areas of South America—of the world—to be fully explored. For although it lies near the Atlantic coast, its terrain and the surrounding rain forest long have insulated the tepuis from intrusion. Some parts remain nearly as remote and strange as Antarctica, dominated by fantasy and legend. Various Indian groups, for example, have lived in tepui country for hundreds of years but have never scaled these mountains, believing them to be the abodes of spirits good and evil. Another myth—that of El Dorado—propelled conquistadores here in a century-long search for the fabled city of Manoa they believed possessed even more riches than already-plundered Peru or Mexico. They never found the city, nor did they breach the defenses of these flat-topped mountains. Neither did their English rival, Sir Walter Raleigh, whose chronic gold fever fueled a lifelong yearning to explore the Caroní River, which drains much of tepui country.

Latter-day treasure hunters include American bush pilot Jimmy Angel, who in the 1930s began to talk of a tepui-top stream he and an old miner worked. "In three days we took 75 pounds of gold out of the gravel," Angel claimed. He spent the rest of his life vainly trying to relocate that fabulous river. In the process, he landed his plane on Auyan-tepui and discovered the waterfall that now bears his name. With 3,212 feet of drop, Angel Falls ranks as the tallest waterfall in the world.

More recently, tepui legends have focused less on mineral riches and more on exotic creatures. Terramar co-founder, biochemist Dr. Fabian Michelangeli, told me about the Makiritare Indian belief in Anakaka—a giant man-ape that supposedly dwells near one of the most southerly tepuis. Wags, Dr. Michelangeli said, have lost no time in nicknaming Anakaka "Tepui-yeti."

Then there is the matter of dinosaurs. The ancient sandstones of tepuis seem far too old for fossils—but not for fantasies. The December 1990 issue of the German magazine GEO—usually nonfiction—features "Search for the Monster," a report that makes Auyan-tepui sound like Loch Ness. The article describes a trip that was inspired by the sighting of a strange animal several years before. Then three men helicoptered to the tepui and spotted a long-necked, saurian-looking creature swimming in a lagoon. All had left their cameras in camp. They went back to retrieve them, and as they returned to the lagoon, the mysterious animal reappeared! By the time they landed, it had vanished, leaving only widening ripples on the water's surface. No footprints, no pictures. I made light of the story, unaware that Fabian's brother, Dr. Armando Michelangeli, a founder and the president of Terramar, was one of the trio. Armando stepped in: "Look. I was *there*. I saw it. It had a head about the size and shape of a rugby football, and a neck about a foot long. It wasn't a river otter because they feed primarily on fish, and there are no fish in that lake. It wasn't a tapir because they can't climb cliffs. What was it? I don't know."

On another trip to Auyan-tepui, however, Terramar scientists turned up tapir tracks. Other scientists have also found them. Armando Michelangeli has even sighted cougars. Perhaps *GEO*'s "monster" *was* a tapir—though no one knows how it got there. At any rate, this is hardly the first dinosaur tale to come out of tepui country. Area resident Alexander Laime claims he saw several long-necked, finned, reptilian creatures one day in 1955, also atop Auyan-tepui. Laime's animals resembled plesiosaurs, only smaller: about three feet long. He was still looking for more of them, four decades later.

In 1912, an Englishman who never visited tepui country but was intrigued by early reports of the area wrote a book relating even more astonishing finds. He called it *The Lost World*. He was Sir Arthur Conan Doyle, creator of Sherlock Holmes. Admittedly fiction, *The Lost World* soon became the classic tale of tepui country; its title remains an apt and oft-used nickname for the region even today. In this boyish adventure, scientists scale a remote tepui—and enter a realm populated by living dinosaurs, apelike "missing links," and other leftovers from a distant past. Nearly impenetrable jungles and sheer cliffs have shielded this tepui so that creatures of post-dinosaur eras never invaded it. Ancient life-forms remained unchallenged, surviving to the present. In effect, chance put a chunk of primeval earth in a bell jar; evolution was thwarted; time stood still.

It's a tale inspired and bolstered by science of the day. As the 19th century ended, Darwin's *On the Origin of Species* had been simmering for decades. Naturalists had just begun to scale tepuis, returning with images of impregnable towers and strange plants that looked like throwbacks to Carboniferous times. Tepuis *were* walled off from the known world by dense forests of the Amazon and the Orinoco. Their sheer sides *did* isolate them even further, also from each other. And they *were* fonts of new species. The fact that resident plants and animals often differed from one tepui to the next fed the notion that these peaks were biological islands, landlocked Galápagos with each tepui cut off from the next as thoroughly as real islands are isolated by ocean. Geologically ancient and biologically "primitive," tepuis became "islands in time." Given this background, it was a relatively small step for Doyle to maroon the most awe-inspiring creatures of earth's geologic past on a singularly secure tepui, insulating them from cataclysms that would doom their brethren elsewhere on the planet.

Fiction but not fantasy, *The Lost World* often apes reality. "It's a good story," tropical ecologist Volkmar Vareschi told me in his Caracas home. The house—like so many in the city—bore a name rather than a number; it was "Tepui." Founder of the school of ecology at Venezuela's Universidad Central and a longtime tepui researcher, this white-haired professor was also a member of Terramar. Dr. Vareschi was one of the first botanists to reach the summit of Auyan-tepui. He recalled, with obvious warmth, the magic of that trip—his first tepui ascent—back in 1956:

"It was another world I found up there. A world of plants which I knew only from books, plants that had existed a long time ago—here they were living still. For example, Rapateaceae and bromeliads—they look something like grasses but belong to other families—dominated this environment. About 20 percent of the plant species we found were endemic; they didn't exist anywhere else. Many were like those in the book of Conan Doyle. But not the animals. There were only frogs and insects, snakes, birds, and other little organisms, not many large species." Even those "minor" animals often included species new to science.

Dr. Otto Huber, like Vareschi a tropical ecologist transplanted from Europe to Venezuela, feels that Doyle's book not only encouraged adventurers and even scientists to probe this exotic area but also influenced some tepui reports.

"They came looking for strange creatures, *expecting* to find them here, largely because of *The Lost World* and the area's isolation," Otto said. "How could a place so remote and different *not* have wonderful, fantastic life-forms?"

Certainly the book influenced Steven Spielberg. Yes, the celebrated maker of celluloid fantasies has been to tepui country, finding it the ideal setting for his thriller *Arachnophobia*. Borrowing from Doyle, his film takes us to a tepui sinkhole where scientists—helicopter-borne, this time—discover not dinosaurs but a new species of spider. It may look like a mere tarantula, but it boasts the jumping ability of a gazelle, venom more lethal than a coral snake's, and the aggressiveness of a pit bull—not to mention rather more intelligence than the movie's humans. The tarantula's existence, like that of Doyle's dinosaurs, hinges directly on the tepui's physical isolation; sheer walls have kept out would-be intruders for ages, shielding resident spiders from all evolutionary starts and stops that have molded life everywhere else.

In reality, however, the impact of physical isolation upon tepui life may be as exaggerated as the gold of El Dorado. Tepuis are not time machines, explains Otto, who has researched many tepuis and also Sierra Maigualida, a curious mountain range in the middle of tepui country. Unlike tepuis, the well-worn Maigualidas are granitic, perhaps an extension of extremely ancient granites that underlie the sandstone tepuis. The Maigualidas rise gradually, in rounded peaks—they are not table mountains.

Their sloped profiles make the Maigualidas accessible to lowland animals and plants. But no jaguars or other large lowland animals have been sighted here—though even the laziest sloth eventually could creep up these mountains if it wanted. Moreover, many plants and animals of the Maigualidas do not differ greatly—some not at all—from those of tepuis. Thus the unique biology of tepuis does not stem solely from physical isolation but, suggests Otto, from chemical poverty of the soils as well as a restrictive climate. Tepui soils, he says, "have almost no nutrients. Plants are growing on SiO_2—silica dioxide—almost pure sand, eroded from the sandstones. See, the Andes are young mountains. They have lots of nutrients. But tepuis have absolutely nothing, only weathered rock. This does not imply that biological communities of tepuis are ancient. No, they are as highly evolved as ones in the Andes. But they have had far fewer opportunities of mixing."

Many tepui species, in fact, are very efficient. Some are highly specialized, securing their nutritional needs directly from the air, from leaf decay, or from insects. Tepuis are not immune to evolution; on the contrary, they have become very finely tuned to their environment by exposure to evolution's pressures over hundreds of millions of years.

Eager to sample tepuis up close, Jay and I buckled into the helicopter with some members of Terramar and headed for Cuquenan-tepui. It rose up like black gauze from lowlands known as La Gran Sabana, "the great savanna," to meet the sky—or at least the cloud cover, shredded and gray. Even in the December-to-March "dry" season, tepuis make their own weather, for they are the first mountains to greet the northeast trades that regularly sweep in from the Caribbean. As we cruised Cuquenan's draped summit, the veil lightened, then broke, revealing dark gray stone fractured into innumerable angular chunks. Not our planned area, but it would do. The pilot dropped through the clouds, putting us down on what could have been a big petrified sponge: black, pocked, and jagged as a lava field. Standing water pooled everywhere. Despite the wet, this place seemed overwhelmingly desertic. Its plants were small, leathery-leaved, spiky: rugged survivors of a challenging realm. And it was incredibly quiet. No birds called, no howler monkeys howled, no other rain forest animals made a sound. Except for the odd butterfly, Cuquenan seemed as devoid of wildlife as peaks three times its 8,695-foot height. All we heard was the soft, haunting wind song sweeping the bleak, rock-strewn plain.

*Remnants of ancient plateaus, tepuis stud the Guiana Highlands, which separate
Venezuela's Orinoco River from the Amazon.*

A stony rise ringed by oddly sculptured boulders and parapets would serve as our campsite. Tiny pineapple-like bromeliads fringed ledges and crannies amid a world of dark stone worked into shapes that played on the mind. Here were pillars, cracked and deeply eroded; top-heavy boulders stacked three or four high; several Easter Island heads, one flung back, its beetled brows, bent nose, protruding lips, and jutting chin bringing to mind the visage of a proud Indian shaman—no doubt displeased by our presence. Countless rock galleries ranged as far as we could see.

Fabian dubbed the cramped campsite *fortaleza,* "fortress," because it was so rock rimmed. In clearing space for our kitchen, someone picked up a stone—and found himself eyeball-to-eyeball with a tarantula. Echoes of Spielberg! But it appeared to be a normal arachnid, living in a hollow beneath the stone that until just now had been its roof. We carefully replaced the rock, opting to share space with this fellow squatter rather than evict it. After all, it was almost the only wildlife we'd seen. And there was no room for a kitchen elsewhere.

Later, Jay and I explored the tepui's broken sprawl. Low ridges split the land into shallow and roughly parallel valleys. Plants somewhat reminiscent of azaleas patterned one corrugated hollow, watered by a stream that alternately narrowed and pooled, creating a series of ponds. Towers of gouged black stone glinted as ever moving clouds continually redirected the sun's beams. Like a Japanese garden, this valley possessed a spare, rugged, but almost calculated wildness.

Beyond, ridges grew progressively higher and more enclosed, evolving into labyrinths with walls 30 or 40 feet high. A snaky stone spout arched out from a bulky base; balanced slabs seemed a house of cards doomed by the next puff of wind. At the tepui's distant edge, broad shelves of rock jutted horizontally from the mountain, deeply undercut by air. More than a mile below lay La Gran Sabana's rumpled mix of green valleys, brownish hills, and grassy vegetation laced by wandering streams. Termite mounds, as regularly spaced as squares of a checkerboard, studded the flats. Not a person was visible, but an obvious pattern of recent fires proved the presence of man.

East of us stood the massive flatiron of Mount Roraima, Cuquenan's sister tepui and the model for Doyle's book. Like Cuquenan, Roraima was flat topped, square shouldered, and blackened with a living skin of algae and lichens. Great rose-colored blotches revealed the sandstone's true color, bared by recent weathering. Jay and I paused. We wanted to ramble even more, but the rock figures around us were running taller, the chasms deeper—and their shadows longer. It was past 5:30. The equatorial sun sets (and rises) notoriously quickly, and Cuquenan's ragged surfaces did not seem likely to forgive many missteps. We turned back toward camp. Evening brought brilliant stars, then clouds, finally mists. Temperatures bottomed barely above freezing—though our latitude was only a few degrees from the Equator. Shivering, we crowded under the kitchen tarp, sharing lentils and rum punch. The tarantula didn't want either.

After a night of misty rain, we awoke to a sodden swirl of white fog and black rock. Roraima, yesterday ablaze in sun, drifted in and out of view while clouds streamed up its vertical face. Weather there was probably even murkier than Cuquenan's, for at an elevation of 9,094 feet Roraima, the easternmost tepui, is the highest in the eastern Venezuela chain, thus bearing the brunt of the trade winds.

A few days later Jay and I stand upon the wet, black moonscape of Roraima's summit. It is barren, craggy, puddled with shallow ponds; a mirror of Cuquenan but on a grander, more fantastic scale. Its surface is cracked more deeply, yielding labyrinths twice as high and far more convoluted, so getting lost—and staying that way—becomes a real danger here, especially when mists turn the sun's disk into a vague, directionless blur. Innumerable stone sculptures, ranging from delicate vanes to massive blocks, deflect winds so crazily that fogs seem to blow simultaneously up *and* down, left *and* right. Drops of condensed water bejewel spiky bromeliads, sticky-fingered sundews, and lichens fringing the rock. It is easy to imagine dinosaurs—and other exotic beasts—alive and well amid such eerie surroundings.

Ahead a tall, narrow object seems to nudge the mists but not quite penetrate them. It is erect, smoothly tapered like . . . the long neck of a brontosaurus. And it is whitish, far too light to match the black slabs all about. I approach cautiously. The mists thin, revealing . . . an obelisk of concrete. Two of its three sides are studded with quartz crystals that spell "Brasil" and "Venezuela." The third is blank but bears a shallow depression; the brass plaque—inscribed "British Guiana"—that originally filled this space had been taken as a souvenir. The obelisk commemorates Roraima's first survey, in 1930, and marks the point where three countries—and three river drainages—meet. Theoretically, at least, a single raindrop hitting the obelisk's exact peak will split three ways, each droplet tracing a path down a different face. Eventually one will enter the Amazon, one the Orinoco, and one the Essequibo—mainstreams respectively of Brazil, Venezuela, and Guyana (no longer British Guiana but an independent nation).

Not far from this triple divide, water has helped sculpture a *foso*—"pit" in Spanish. It is oval, perhaps 60 feet across at its widest, 20 feet deep, as sheer-walled as a cook pot. A shallow and crystalline lagoon, fed by a waterfall of surface streams tumbling freely over the foso's edge, floors its bottom. One rare sunny day, hot from scrambling over Roraima's rocks, we could not resist this pool's allure. Off went the clothes. One of our Terramar companions rigged up a cable ladder, and down the slick sandstone we went, one at a time, like ants. The water—surprisingly icy—came hardly to my knees but took my breath away. I thrashed across its surface to where one wall had been undercut into a cavern of natural arches. Instead of stalactites, living ferns billowed down from the rock. The cave narrowed to a slit, then opened into a second chamber, lit by a hole in the rock roof and carpeted with a sand beach. It was wonderfully secluded, totally unexpected. After rambling a while, I went back up the ladder—and shook involuntarily for the next 20 minutes, even after dressing and sitting in welcome sunshine. Yes, you can get frostbite on the Equator—without daring to Andean heights. Another surprise was blood flowing freely down elbows and knuckles. Though I'd felt nothing, Roraima's extremely abrasive sandstone had flayed my skin—painlessly, thanks to the lagoon's frigidly anesthetizing waters.

Fosos occur commonly on tepuis, though sandstone is far less soluble than limestone, the usual medium for caves and sinks. Apparently, the numerous fractures that crosshatch tepui surfaces often run deep; water enters, weakens the "glue" holding particles of sand together, and speeds collapse of rock along the fractures, widening them and encouraging further erosion. Over time, sizable passages maze the stone, eventually breaking through in visible waterfalls. Were it not for this foso's leaky bottom, its waterfall would have filled it to the brim long ago.

Given the right conditions, a foso becomes a sinkhole—a sheer-sided and flat-bottomed shaft. Some reach enormous proportions; Aonda sinkhole on Auyan-tepui yawns about a thousand feet long and more than a thousand feet down—nearly as deep as the Empire State Building is high. The Terramar group we have been traveling with includes several climbers eager to descend Aonda.

So it is that I find myself on Auyan-tepui one morning, in the company of Raul, Wilman, Mono, Edgar, and Marcus as they load on climbing gear and strike out through water-filled bromeliads and spiky scrub trees. Almost immediately, we get lost. Raul, here years ago, can't recall the route at first, but soon has us back on track. A rolling gait—the sort useful in deep snow—seems to work well in the underbrush, though the sharp trees claw ceaselessly at arms and legs. Fifteen minutes of this takes us to the edge of the sinkhole. Horizontally, Aonda's outline is a teardrop; we stand near the narrow end. Vertically, the sinkhole seems bottomless—though lead climber Raul assures me it is "only" 1,214 feet deep. He plans the group's descent along three sequential drops. First comes a 656-foot vertical wall. Then the rock retreats, creating a 361-foot "dangle" without handholds or footholds; climbers will just hang in the air from their ropes. The final leg takes in a mere 197 feet, along a steep but not vertical shelf.

At once we search for a spot to anchor the climbing rope. Dense shrubbery and few visible rock outcrops make direct tie to stone difficult, so Raul ties in to several *trees,* whose trunks range in diameter from six inches to only an inch. Worse yet, they are mired in mucky soil at the sinkhole's edge; one tug of the rope could set everything in motion. I am aghast, but no one else seems concerned. Wilman cheerfully bolsters Raul's work with a few more knots and bits of rope and webbing, all the time singing "La Donna è Mobile," from *Rigoletto.* Soon the others are whistling along in four-part harmony. These guys are about to drop off a thousand-foot cliff, and they're *elated.*

Yet only a week ago, most of those here today took part in a sinkhole descent on Cuquenan that ended badly. One climber, Samuel, less experienced than his teammates, lost control of his rappel rig about 40 yards from the bottom and kept accelerating, nearly free-falling by the time he smashed into the sinkhole's bottom, jamming one thigh bone through his hip. He easily could have perished. But our helicopter pilot ventured to the very bottom of that remote, steep-walled pit—despite close quarters, despite winds bouncing off surrounding walls, despite cloud cover—and retrieved the injured man. Many other pilots would never contemplate such a flight. Samuel was lucky.

I look again at the spider's nest of rope and webbing that serves as anchor today, and shake my head. Raul puts on a pair of climbing shoes so ragged they could almost pass for sandals, then ropes in, backs to the edge of the pit, and suddenly steps off—with a joyous and feisty hoot that is his personal talisman. He is instantly out of sight; the rope tautens—and holds. I hear the low whine of metal on nylon as he glides into the abyss, his rappel rack keeping his descent at manageable speed. I cannot see him, but a walkie-talkie keeps us in radio contact. For now, all is well.

Wilman, still whistling, is next. He carries a second rope, coiled, which he and Raul will fix near the bottom of the initial overhang for the second drop. To watch their progress, I must go to the sinkhole's far side. Reluctantly. I slog again through the shin-bashing bromeliads, jabbing shrubs, and algae-slick rocks that edge the sinkhole. Soon some bare, flat-topped boulders appear, affording prime views. Aonda is simply stunning. Its vertical, fluted walls match one side to the other, as if the rock just split apart one day like the San Andreas Fault. Sides parallel each other nearly all the way down, spawning a profile far different from the Grand Canyon's stepped "V"—though water formed both. Narrow rock ledges nudge out from the vertical, giving rise to cascades of greenery rooted there and hanging down into the abyss.

While I admire these living cataracts, the corner of my eye spots a multihued spider inching down its silken thread. No, it's Wilman! On the dangle, suspended by a swaying nylon lifeline. Already he is halfway to the sinkhole's forested bottom. Tonight he and two others will bed down there; tomorrow, all will safely return by the same ropes, using mechanical ascenders. Time to celebrate—and to return to civilization.

We load the chopper a final time and take off from Auyan's top, the pilot gradually descending as he follows the Carrao River. Locals call it a "blackwater" stream because it is stained dark brown by tannins from decaying leaves. Closer and closer looms the Carrao, and in a flash its bottom falls out. Black water instantly turns white: The river erupts in a battery of side-by-side waterfalls, together low and broad like Niagara, gleamingly white in the sun. Nearby swirls a large, curving lagoon, rimmed by sandy beach and a sweep of thatched roofs belonging to a resort hotel. A scattering of tepuis forms the perfect backdrop. To eyes that have just spent two weeks in the wet and stony never-never land of tepui country, this idyllic scene seems more mirage than real. We circle several times, as if to certify it exists. On the way to the helipad we pass tractors towing open carts painted in tiger stripes and crammed with tourists—and I realize it's no mirage. This is Canaima, "gateway to the Lost World." Our adventure with Terramar has come to an end. Jay and I will explore Canaima on our own.

It does not take us long to tour the town. A ten-minute walk along potholed roads of dusty red dirt takes us from hotel to airstrip, past guide services and souvenir shops and a tiny residential core, to the compound of C.V.G. EDELCA, the regional government utility. That's it.

The hotel is not as idyllic as it first appeared. Meals here are steam-table cafeteria fare, rooms are cramped, and the placid lagoon is not recommended for swimming because of a persistent sewage disposal problem. The resort belongs to AVENSA, Venezuela's largest privately owned airline, and it will not book passage for you to Canaima unless you also pay for one night at its hotel. Jay and I opt for a kinder, gentler hostelry just upriver from the falls. It is Ucaima Camp, operated by Rudy Truffino—a transplanted Hollander who has been in the region since the mid-1950s. Rudy, in fact, began the Canaima resort, but later lost out to AVENSA, and started over in Ucaima.

Bearded, thin as a rail, quick with a smile, Rudy kept only eight rooms, valuing relaxed atmosphere over higher revenues. Currasows and other native birds freely roamed the grounds among his cabins. We were in the main building only a few minutes before Tru-tru, a rain forest oriole about the size and color of a mynah, flew in and alighted on my shoulder. "Don't worry," said Rudy. "Just look out for your eyes." I did, while Rudy offered Tru-tru dabs of marmalade, then Coke. Both were gobbled up. "I raised him," Rudy added with pride. "I raised all the birds here from eggs. When they grow up, I clip the wings once, and that's it. No pens or leashes. They go anywhere they want."

At breakfast the next day, a pair of toucans appeared at our table.

"Tutti and Frutti," Rudy announced. "The male is Tutti and the female is Frutti. She's a bit more colorful."

Quickly a large woodpecker with a red crest showed up, then irrepressible Tru-tru. He wasted no time with pleasantries, just plopped on the table and started pecking away at Rudy's omelet. The doting host opened a jar of the bird's favorite and, in seconds, Tru-tru's beak was smothered in Cheez Whiz.

Across the well-kept lawn trotted Bambi—a *matacan*, or jungle deer, the size of a big spaniel. "She always comes by, licks the dog, and sleeps with it," Rudy explained. His obvious love for animals reflected a veterinary background. That plus a lifelong yen for unconventional places and life-styles brought him to Venezuela after forays at farming (in Tunisia) and tending polo ponies (in the Dominican Republic). Eventually Rudy and his wife, Gerti, settled in the bush of the Lost World, becoming guides and hoteliers, while rearing three daughters and living out their jungle dream.

Recalled Rudy, "There was nobody here when we came in, just three Indian families behind those mountains. All the Indians you see today came from the east over the last ten or fifteen years. We used to have jaguar, puma, ocelot, anaconda, boa, bushmaster, a whole bunch of snakes. Also tapir, *chiguire* (capybara), all that stuff. But not any more."

Indeed, human impacts now reach even to the tepui tops. Volkmar Vareschi, the ecologist so entranced by Auyan-tepui on his first visit 35 years ago, told me of more recent events:

"Yes, there have been changes. A fire was accidentally started by the helpers of a botanist on Auyan-tepui. And Roraima—the most visited tepui and the easiest to climb—has been damaged very badly. There have been many tourists."

Graffiti, he added, now mark some Roraima rocks. And a shallow valley on its summit, once crammed with geodes and large quartz crystals that fueled enduring tales of the area's vast mineral wealth, has been totally plundered.

"People destroyed the crystals," said Vareschi. "Took them off in bags, and left their trash up there. With their boots came plants like *Plantago*—what Indians call 'the footsteps of the white man.' It never existed up there before, but now it does."

Such intrusions may seem minor in a place so remote and historically little used by man. But Otto Huber points out, "Tepuis are unique laboratories of nature, outstanding both in plant life and topography, in the middle of the tropical zone. Where else can you find such mountains, never occupied or modified by a human population?

"No other region in the world has these kinds of ecosystems at that elevation. It's all table mountains, jutting up very abruptly. This creates a whole series of ecosystems over a short distance. Sloped mountains usually have gradual transitions from one life zone to the next. On tepuis you have two or three abrupt steps, and each has evolved in its own direction, without all the genetic interchange that normally occurs among neighboring life communities. You find more strange things, in very little space."

Tepuis, Otto adds, now need man's help to survive. For though their unique vegetation may seem lush and rugged, often it is highly fragile, with recovery limited by slow growth rates.

Not surprisingly, he lobbies energetically for tepui preservation. "If we really want to maintain certain areas of the world as pristine," he says, "this should be a core area. There are very few environments in South America so well suited for this purpose. *Nobody* lives on the tepuis. So, with little effort, they could be kept pristine and remain the biological labs they always have been, continuing their course of evolution undisturbed by man."

More and more people, however, now want to visit them. Adventurers—not only climbers and trekkers but also sky divers, parasailors, balloonists, and others—increasingly seek their thrills in tepui country. One lunatic even bicycled off Auyan-tepui (with a parachute) in hope of winning mention in the *Guinness Book of World Records*. (He survived the jump, but failed to make it into the book.) While few adventurers intend to harm tepuis, many wind up doing just that.

But Otto remains optimistic, partly for economic reasons. "Very few tepuis are really exploitable for tourism," he says. "Many are just a wall with some forest beneath."

Vareschi cautions, "People—travelers, adventurers—will always want to get on the tepuis. You can't stop them, but there should be scientific investigation of all tepuis with all possible speed, to see what exists in these places—before they change. Secondly, we could commit one or two tepuis to tourist use. Like the Galápagos—there are islands where tourists can go on paths marked for them, and there are islands where it is forbidden to step. It should be the same here."

On paper at least, Venezuela has set aside all tepuis, either as part of 7.5 million-acre Canaima National Park, or as individual natural monuments that amount to an additional 5 million acres. But are these reserves safe?

In 1990 tepuis and Canaima National Park accounted for about 70 percent of the Venezuelan national park system. Deud Dumith, president of Inparques—the Venezuelan bureau of national parks—told me: "They are unique ecosystems, attractive to tourism but at the same time quite fragile. And tourism is increasing very rapidly. Visitor levels definitely are a major problem. Tepuis require even more protection now."

Although Canaima National Park was given World Heritage Status in 1994, it continues to be managed on a shoestring budget: the operational management allocation for the Eastern sector during 1996 was $1,171. And the tourism industry, which almost doubled between 1991 and 1995, continues to develop within the park without sufficient planning control.

C.V.G. EDELCA, the utility, intends near-total development of the Caroni River watershed. Already it has built Guri Dam, currently one of the world's largest hydroelectric projects. Although EDELCA has shown concern for the environment, it plans four more dams for the Caroni, including one that may inundate part of Canaima National Park. Completion is scheduled for 2004.

Warns Otto Huber, "Then the 'islands in time' will be *real* islands."

Dumith downplays the threat. "C.V.G. EDELCA will have to convince people to justify these constructions. I can't ensure that the dam won't be built. But it will be very difficult, politically. In the past, politicians thought 'protection' was a kind of idealism. Now they are aware that in national parks we have our major resources. So conservation is a business, an investment."

My Venezuela adventure was at an end. I would leave tepui country as I'd found it—its future uncertain. If Dumith, Huber, and others convince politicians to make an investment here, Venezuela's Lost World just might share a common feature of Spielberg's many films: a happy ending.

If not, this enduring realm of legend and adventure could become truly lost.

Home stretch: The last of four climbers inches up the lip of a sinkhole on Cuquenan. A fifth climber broke a hip on the descent but lived; a daring pilot helicoptered into the abyss to rescue him.

FOLLOWING PAGES: Roraima's waterlogged corrugations point toward Cuquenan—and attest to age-old erosion that has riddled its seemingly flat top with countless clefts, pinnacles, and mazes.

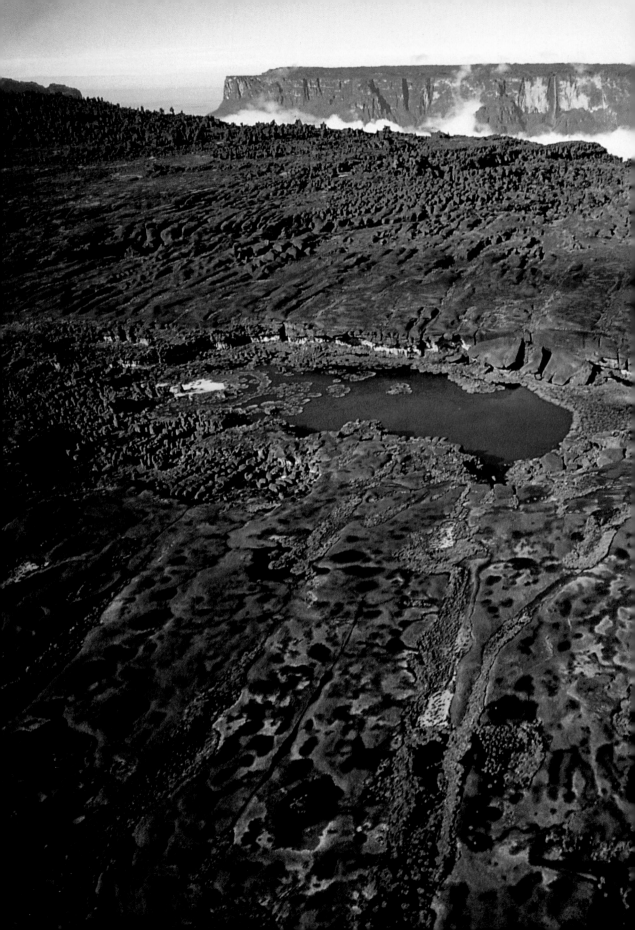

Ultimate badlands: Cloaked in mists and fractured into innumerable passageways, Roraima's skin offers a rock climber endless possibilities. Once avoided by man, tepuis now attract tourists, adventurers, and vandals—and increasingly suffer the pressures of human presence.

*F*ramed by a Venezuelan version of Monument Valley, Terramar limnologists—pond and lake specialists—sample a natural cistern on Cuquenan (opposite) to determine the water's dissolved nutrients and microscopic life. Lichens and algae blacken the tepui's pink sandstones and quartzites, enhancing the stark, forbidding look of this land. Amid scenes like this lurk biological curiosities such as tiny Oreophrynella (above)—a toad that neither hops nor swims—and snakes such as Thamnodynastes (top), at home in the granitic Sierra Maigualida of southern Venezuela.

Winged but flightless species of water cricket—as yet unnamed by science—fights the current of a stream creasing Acopan-tepui (below); dark Stigonema algae mottle the pale rock. Lower and more sheltered than Roraima or Cuquenan, Acopan harbors different life-forms. Sphagnum mosses soften a glen where insect larvae freckle submerged stone (opposite).

FOLLOWING PAGES: Sunshot profiles of great stone faces guard Cuquenan's deeply eroded roof. Endless variations both fascinate and deceive the eye; labyrinths that appear low-walled often rise higher than expectations, disorienting trekkers, while the crumbly stone offers poor handholds.

*F*lamboyant rainbow of tepui life flaunts bizarre shapes and textures as well as colors.
A caterpillar munches a leaf (below), and a brilliant Kunhardtia rhodantha *flower head (bottom)*
awaits fertilization by hummingbirds. Cherry red nectariums of Heliamphora nutans—*"sun pitcher"*
(opposite)—exude a perfume alluring to insects; downward-pointing hairs ease victims into the
pitchers, where they drown and become food for the plant. Highly adapted over eons, tepui plants and
animals often exist on a single mountain or massif; related but different species inhabit other tepuis.

Bit of Eden hellishly named, verdant Cañón del Diablo—"devil's canyon"—punctuates rugged Auyan-tepui with a serpentine recess of primeval rain forest that feeds the Churun River.

FOLLOWING PAGES: World's tallest cataract—Angel Falls—cascades 3,212 feet down an Auyan-tepui cliff, turning from torrent to mist by the time it hits bottom. Its name stems not from divine beings but from an earthier source: American bush pilot Jimmy Angel, first to land atop Auyan.

*R*oofed by sky, teardrop-shaped Aonda sinkhole (above) plummets more than a thousand feet
into the heart of Auyan-tepui, ever luring thrill seekers to take the plunge. Sheer scarps
and daunting overhangs shrink an intruding helicopter to gypsy moth proportions, while a climber's
spidery rope traces a nearby wall (opposite). Although airborne excursions to tepuis and
sinkholes require special permits, unauthorized flights do occur—prompting concerns about visitor
safety, noise pollution, and increasing degradation of this unique natural resource.

FOLLOWING PAGES: Stair-step ramparts of Auyan-tepui ascend into gathering cloud,
evoking illusions of a natural Shangri-la: pristine, wild, totally isolated from human cares.

AUSTRALIA

SONG LINE OF THE KIMBERLEY

Stupendous tides wash the ragged coast of the Kimberley,
a largely empty sprawl of rugged mountains, remote plateaus,
and deep gorges in Australia's far north.

By Christine Eckstrom   Photographed by Paul Chesley

I stand on the bow of the boat like a scout, breathing warm air blown from the hot land, as we enter a great cleft in the coast of northwestern Australia, a winding red passage leading into the ancient red continent. Flanking the channel are steep cliffs of naked rock, formed of sandstone hundreds of millions of years old, fractured into great blocks, tilted and tumbled, like the walls of a ruined temple. The cliffs grow higher and narrower the farther upriver we travel, and it seems the passage leads not only deeper into the continent but also back into a long-vanished era on earth. In the waters below, silken and clear, huge lavender jellyfish drift by, pulsing through the inverted reflections of the ancient cliffs. The dark forms of big fish cruise slowly beneath them, and in coves of tangled mangroves along the banks, deep grooves in the mud and murky swirls near shore reveal the places where crocodiles have slid undersea in advance of our approach.

It is strangely quiet in this saltwater canyon, eerie in the absence of any sign of man. This is the continent as the first European explorers would have seen it three centuries ago, as the ancestors of the first Aborigines might have seen these shores when they reached them nearly 50,000 years before. So primordial and untouched does the scene appear that I feel I am in the presence of a land so old it holds stories of ages beyond reckoning, yet so newly found it awaits human imagination to give its creation a tale.

Miles upstream, the passage ends at a wall where a river from the interior falls in a thin sheet down to the sea. Atop perches a Brahminy kite, guarding the way to the lands beyond, its white head illumined in the sun, its majestic appearance like a reward for those who reach this hidden place. We anchor nearby, watching the last line of sunlight edge up the cliffs, leaving blackened walls of night behind. In this silent canyon out of time, I feel like the first soul

Aswirl against Cape Voltaire, Indian Ocean surf churns an agate reflection of seaside palisades in the rugged and remote Kimberley, a 125,000-square-mile region in northwestern Australia.

PRECEDING PAGES: *King Cascade stairsteps 160 feet down sandstone terraces hung with ferns along the Prince Regent River. At low tide a boat drifts at anchor; high tide raises the water level 20 feet.*

DAVID DOUBILET (PRECEDING PAGES)

on the continent, drifting to sleep beneath the arch of the Milky Way, listening to the stillness and the murmur of stars.

I have come to this place on a land-and-sea journey through the region known as the Kimberley, one of the wildest and least known areas on the island continent, and one that even few Australians have seen. For me it was an odyssey of adventure and discovery, guided by the imaginings of those who came before—explorers and settlers and the first Aborigines—and by a measure of traveler's serendipity and the urge to find what lies in places where others seldom go.

Kimberley country is big, covering an area the size of California on the northwest shoulder of Australia, but with a small-town population of only 30,000 people, most of whom live in settlements along its fringes. Geographically, the Kimberley stands apart, bordered by the red reaches of the Northern Territory to the east, the Great Sandy Desert to the south, and the rocking waters of the Indian Ocean and the Timor Sea on its western and northern shores. The land within these bounds is a dramatic confusion of geology, a high-plateau country crenellated with snaking mountain ranges that rise to heights of 3,000 feet and tortuous with mazes of plunging gorges and seasonal rivers that twist crazily down to the sea.

Climate has conspired with topography to keep the region little populated and under-explored. For most of the year the Kimberley is as dry as a desert, but during the annual monsoon season known as the Wet, thunderous storms sweep the land. From January to March an average of three feet of rain falls, turning a red country green and filling toe-deep streams with waters that crest in 40-foot-high floods and rush to the sea over waterfalls like the one where the Brahminy kite sat watching us.

It was August, the height of the Dry, when I set off with photographer Paul Chesley on a voyage down the Kimberley coast. The skies were cloudless and blue up north in the austral winter, and rivers like the one where we anchored had dropped and receded into chains of billabongs—cool, deep pools of permanent water as delightful as the sound of their name. Aboard the *Dawn Star II,* a 42-foot fishing boat, we left the port town of Wyndham in the northeast Kimberley and headed for Broome, a small city west then south around the corner of the continent, nearly 900 zigzagging sea miles away. With us were wilderness guide Mike Osborn, skipper Eric Parker, and first mate Robert "Blue" Vaughan. All three were Australians, all were avid fishermen, and none had ever traveled farther by sea down the Kimberley coast than the wild, red canyon we reached the first night.

The Timor Sea was a madness of wind and waves when we left the red passage the following day to head west for the Indian Ocean. Whitecaps danced as far as the eye could see, and we entered the sea with a lurch. Pots and utensils flew in the galley, waves sprayed the decks, chairs and coolers slid wildly to one side on the open stern.

All day long the boat rocked and pitched, surfing down waves into troughs, slipping sideways like a slalom skier out of control, then heaving up again to the next precarious crest as the coast of Australia bobbed up and down on the far horizon. The boat seemed too small for this ocean. Paul buried his cameras in blankets, Mike and Blue despaired of a chance to fish, but from the wheel on the flying bridge Eric cried like a pirate, "Aar! I love the sea."

I thought of the first explorers. In the early 1600s, when European maps of the world showed a landmass labeled *Terra Australis Incognita*—a huge southern continent only imagined to exist—a Dutch skipper en route to Java accidentally landed on the coast of western Australia, though far to the south of the Kimberley. Dirk Hartog came ashore on October 25, 1616, the first European to set foot on the continent. He nailed a pewter plate to a post to mark his visit and sailed on, believing he had discovered some uninhabited isles.

For the rest of that century, Dutch flags flew atop most of the European vessels that cruised into the strange new waters of Australia. Ship captains heading from Amsterdam to a colonial base in the East Indies found they could cut their travel time in half by sailing the swift winds across the southern Indian Ocean due east from Africa's Cape of Good Hope before turning north for Java. In so doing, many of them sailed a bit too far east, into Australia. Some wrecked, some landed, some looked around a bit. "A barren accursed earth," one captain wrote in 1629.

The Dutch sent Abel Tasman off to explore. In 1644, he sailed the entire shoreline of northern Australia and halfway down the western side of the continent, becoming the first European to see the Kimberley coast. His maps, to this day, are remarkably accurate, but his log has mysteriously disappeared. All that remains of Tasman's record of that journey is the binder that once held his journals.

I longed to know the impressions Tasman had of the Kimberley as we traveled along in his wake, his accomplishment seeming all the more heroic as the ocean tossed us down the coast. We rose and fell past miles of high, rolling tablelands that drop sheer to the sea in orange layer-cake cliffs, some clean-sliced, some broken off in avalanche piles of chunks the size of houses. It looked as if, in places, the coast had exploded. We saw no boats, no towns, no settlements. The Kimberley shores had surely looked to Tasman exactly as they looked to us.

From the second day, mother nature and the nature of the coast changed our plans to leisurely cruise the Kimberley, stopping here and there to hike inland. Rough seas forced Eric to steer us farther offshore, away from hazards not marked on the charts—shifting sand shoals rippling with shallow breakers and half-submerged rock piles where waves burst skyward in arcs of foam.

We abandoned plans to travel at night. Eric's charts—the best to be had—showed too many areas along the coast striped in red and marked "Unsurveyed waters." In one case, a zone we had to pass through was ominously labeled "Former mined area." At times it seemed Tasman's maps would have served us well; I remember Eric hollering once, chart in hand at the wheel, "This shows *two* islands—*two!* There's *ten* bloody islands out there."

For several days we traveled hard to make up for lost nighttime miles, starting at first light and stopping just before dusk to find a calm place to anchor—and fish. Mike landed several fresh dinners, and Eric spent long evenings at the stern pulling up squid with a handline and releasing sharks from casting poles. But if we all harbored secret ideas of what we might find on this journey, it was Blue whose hopes were most single-minded and determined. As a longtime pursuer of a wily Australian fish known as the barramundi—big and delicious and famed in the Kimberley as the quintessential finned fighter—Blue dreamed of discovering somewhere on this long, ragged, wild coast the unknown but ultimate "Barramundi Bay," a name he optimistically christened each place we dropped anchor.

Blue himself was festooned with fishing charms. Every day he wore a windbreaker checkered with fishing club patches and his old lucky hat, the band prickly with hooks and lures and pins showing leaping barramundi, the underside of the brim painted green—with a toothbrush—to reduce the glare of sunlight passing through the straw while Blue scanned the waters for fish. His tackle box overflowed with an angler's museum of barramundi lures that rattle, twirl, and skip in the water. Blue hunted barramundi at every opportunity, puttering off in the dinghy to cast in secluded nooks and coves, and one glorious time he hooked one. "Barramundi this big," he said, spreading his arms wide as he stepped back on board. "Got a hit, a hook up—couple of jumps, under a rock, broke the line. Saw him take the lure."

The barramundi is the perfect Kimberley fish, thriving in all manner of waters—fresh, salt, and brackish—but requiring access to the sea, where it spawns. It's finicky, it fights hard, and it's big—reaching weights of nearly 90 pounds. From all over Australia—and beyond—

serious fishermen come to the Kimberley in quest of barramundi, and one night I asked Blue how the fish had hooked him. "It's their elusiveness," he said, "and they're a beautiful fish. A polished aluminum color with big scales—big for their size—and red-orange eyes. It's the eyes, I think," he continued, gazing off. "They glow, even in the daytime, and you can see them in the dark, shining in the water like crocodile eyes. Beautiful they are, like hot coals."

Blue was watching the evening Mike and I set off in the dinghy to cast into a rippling patch of sea where a school of fish was racing by. Bam, *z-z-z-z,* a fish hit my lure and zipped off with a tug and a great burst of speed. I reeled, and it ran in looping circles and beelines until I finally pulled it in—a 20-pound Spanish mackerel, the biggest fish we would land on the trip, and a fine dinner that night. To me, the catch was a lucky surprise, but it was more so to Blue when he saw my tackle—a hook and a marble-size marabou jig on nylon 12-pound test line. "Those fish have teeth like knives!" he said. "If I told my mates in Perth you caught that fish with no wire leader, they'd tell me, 'Aw nick off, mate.' I'm genuinely happy for you," Blue added, "but I'd be dark if that was a barramundi."

The seas grew calmer after we rounded three tempestuous capes and angled southwestward into Indian Ocean waters, cruising in the sheltering lee of the Bonaparte Archipelago, a long arc of rocky isles that buffered the force of the waves. We edged in closer to shore, easing along tall cliffs whose seaside faces bore the fearsome tattoo of the Kimberley coast—an even, dark line, muddy and encrusted with mollusks, reaching from sea level far up the rocks. It is the high-water mark of daily tides that may rise and fall a monstrous 40 feet—the highest in the Southern Hemisphere—making the Kimberley among the most dangerous coasts in the world to navigate and leaving much of its shoreline too treacherous for ports, too restless for settlement.

One enthusiastic romantic who thought the Kimberley coast might make a fine place for colonization was Sir George Grey, who explored the Prince Regent River region of the central Kimberley coast in 1837–38. He arrived just before the rains began and set off inland on foot. He was barely able to scale the cliffs, so steep and burning hot were the rocks; his dogs disappeared in crevasses the first day; his party nearly died of thirst; and he nearly drowned in a violent tidal surge. He was plagued by bush flies, attacked by stinging ants, speared by Aborigines. Grey pressed on, incurably enchanted by the beauty of the wilderness. After five months of "toils and sufferings," he concluded, surprisingly, that the area, though it "offered almost insurmountable difficulties to first explorers," was "admirably adapted for both commerce and agriculture."

The waters were rising, and we all stood silently on the bow as Eric steered us through a fast-flowing funnel between tall fjord walls into the basin at the mouth of the Prince Regent River, the Kimberley's most majestic portal to the interior—and a place that is as much a wilderness now as it was when Grey roamed here a century and a half ago. To the north rose two massive buttes, like great ships riding high on a stormy sea of land, and all around stretched long vistas of broken hills and red-bouldered country.

From a glassy anchorage upriver, Mike, Paul, and I set off to explore in the dinghy, poking up tiny tributaries impenetrable with mangroves, finally finding one that led to a wide cascade where, for the first time since we headed out to sea, we set foot on land. We hiked up inland, climbing the stream's winding staircase of rocks, passing pool after lovely pool—river billabongs, serene and blue and blanketed with lily pads. Paperbark trees shaded the shores, their white trunks shaggy with patches of peeling bark that, inside, feels as soft as suede. At high noon, high up, at a deep, round billabong circled with boulders, we jumped in for a swim, drinking from a cold, rushing waterfall, watching flocks of white cockatoos soar overhead—as carried away by the charm of the wilderness as Grey had once been.

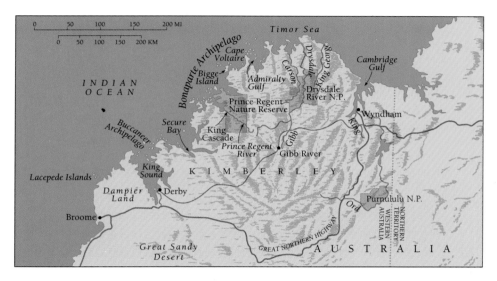

Much of Kimberley country's wilderness coastline, ocher cliffs, and rugged hills remain unexplored.

But a wilderness in our time is usually still wild for a reason, and Kimberley beauty always has a catch. When we returned to the dinghy, the falling tide—still dropping—had stranded it in mud, knee-deep and slimy-slick. We struggled to free it, slipping and stumbling, and just as we shoved it afloat, Mike cautioned, "Hop in—quickly—don't want to see you taken."

"Taken" is the euphemism Australians use for being attacked by a crocodile, and the finality implied is appropriate. "Once a big croc's got you, that's it," said Mike. "They take you down underwater and out of sight—there's not much anyone can do. Then they wedge you up under a rock or a log until," he paused, "well—until you're soft enough for a chew. They're not choosy," he added, almost brightly. "They'll take kangaroos, cows—anything that happens to come along."

Kimberley country is often described as "crocodile-infested," although the freshwater variety found in interior waters—affectionately, "freshies"—usually pose no threat to people. It is the saltwater crocodiles Mike described—unaffectionately, "salties"—that give the species its dreadful reputation. They are man-eaters, and the waters of the Kimberley coast are one of their last great strongholds. While fears and tales of crocs, like those of sharks, may be exaggerated—the death toll is about one a year in Australia—the once-overhunted salties are now protected, and as their numbers increase, so does their danger to the unwary.

The Prince Regent has plenty of salties, and they loomed large in our imaginations. We saw their tail slides and claw marks along the banks, and we always knew they were there—camouflaged in the mud among the prop roots of mangroves, drifting motionless with mats of floating debris, lying torpid on the murky river bottom, or crouched low in the shallows, awaiting whatever creature comes close enough. Salties strike with an explosive lunge and a slam of jaws. Though they are often unseen, their existence occupies the same niche in the mind as lions and leopards in Africa, polar bears in the Arctic—it's their country, and you follow their rules.

I had spotted my first saltie a few days earlier, ironically, just as I was about to bend a rule and take a quick dip from the stern. A medium-size 13-footer—they can reach lengths of

20 feet—he cruised slowly past the boat, in tempting turquoise shallows, forever ending any thoughts of saltwater swimming. In the Prince Regent we avoided even visiting a waterfall where, in 1987, a young American woman was "taken." Mike, who worked for 17 years as a wildlife officer in Western Australia, has wide-ranging experience with capturing and translocating salties. "Crocs lead a pretty casual life," he said. "They just lie around and wait. Big ones can go for months without eating, but when they decide to have a go, they don't waste their energy unless they're sure of success. And," he added, "they rarely miss."

That night we anchored around the bend of the Prince Regent entrance, at the very place where Grey had launched his explorations. His 1838 report makes little mention of crocodiles, but the settlers who came here in 1864—inspired by Grey's account—encountered them, along with every other conceivable Kimberley hazard: drought, flood, flies, fever, sunstroke. One of their ships wrecked on the rocks; tides swept most of their provisions out to sea; and they abandoned the site less than a year later. A few graves are all that remain of their short-lived presence, small monuments to a vision shattered—and a wilderness resistant.

Wondrous creatures, like signs, began to appear at sea in the days after we left the Prince Regent. Flying fish skimmed over the waves, and fleets of jellyfish floated by; banded sea snakes, striped yellow and black, wriggled along on the surface, mouths agape; now and then, green turtles popped up their heads for breath—and disappeared. Schools of dolphins escorted us for a while, then pods of humpback whales joined in, breaching and diving around the boat—bursting up from the sea, smashing down with great booms, and spouting tall geysers of spray that caught the slant of the sun and made rainbows.

Finally, they waved off with their flukes, or so it seemed, as we turned south into the waters of the Buccaneer Archipelago, where, scattered around on every horizon, were scores of isles of fantastic form—some tilted like sinking ships, some rising like gargantuan sand castles, and others with sheer pink cliffs, broken off on seams like calving icebergs. Two hundred islands and reefs make up the archipelago, and it was named to honor the English explorer-buccaneer William Dampier, who, with Tasman's charts in hand, sailed through these islands on two daring voyages in the late 1600s. On returning to England, he penned a book of such fabulous adventure that his accounts captured not only the public's fancy but also the attention of writer Jonathan Swift, who alluded to his creative debt to "my cousin Dampier" in the introductory pages of Gulliver's Travels—and mapped his fictional lands of Lilliput and Blefuscu as newly found isles off the western coast of Australia.

Enough days and distance had passed that the journey began to take on a mythical quality, and in the seas through the Buccaneers we entered a passage reminiscent of Gulliver's trials at sea. Suddenly, all around us, the water began to spin with whirlpools, swirling and gurgling and bubbling up from below as if the sea were about to boil. The entire ocean was patterned with contrary waves and cyclone-shaped whorls that jostled us from side to side, jolting like an earthquake and skidding the boat so uncontrollably that, at times, we traveled sideways—and backward. It was the outgoing tide, building up in water walls against the natural barrier of the islands and rushing between them in powerful surges, creating audible suctions and colliding currents. When Eric saw hidden reefs and rocks suddenly rise up— exposed by the falling tide—we turned around and headed back out to open sea, where it seemed, as in a fable, the whales hadn't been waving us off, but beckoning us to go.

Around the peninsula of Dampier Land, with Broome one sea-day away, we made a small detour off the southwest Kimberley to stop at the Lacepede Islands, a cluster of sandy isles low and nearly lost in the sea. For ages uncounted the islands have been a compass-center for creatures of the seas and the skies. Frigatebirds, sooty terns, brown boobies, and green sea turtles—hallmark fauna of warm, wild seacoasts—home in on the tiny Lacepedes to nest. We headed off to see what wild things were sojourning there.

Three brown boobies flapped along in our wake, then more appeared, in ever increasing numbers, soaring in long skeins and V's, returning home for the night. We anchored off one of the Lacepedes, a thin white line on the ocean, under a great swirling dome of birds that peppered the skies, high up and far off to every horizon. Frigatebirds glided above clouds of brown boobies, and flocks of sooty terns circled up from the island in funnels as we pulled the dinghy ashore on a sloping beach crisscrossed with tractor-tread trails and pocked with deep craters—the telltale tracks and nests of sea turtles.

We hiked up to the top of the beach, where, spaced evenly along the grasses lining the sand, sat young booby chicks, downy and white as snowmen, their black eyes fixed on us. I peered beyond them, into the island's interior, to meet the gaze of thousands of eyes—white chicks to the end of the isle, fluffy whitecaps in a rolling sea of brown tussocks, each seated alone in its own flattened grass clearing, looking startled and curious, all staring at me as their parents swooped in to join them.

Among the birds and the tracks of the turtles, we watched the sunset blaze orange as the moon rose full—a crescendo night of the month for sea life. Though by the books it was not the nesting season, the tracks on the beach were so numerous and fresh that we decided to come back for a night turtle watch. While we were on board preparing to return, amid our elation over what we had already seen, magic succeeded magic. The skies grew strangely darker, and we looked up to see the shadow of the earth eclipse the moon.

The moon reappeared and illuminated the white beach like a stage. Stepping ashore, we tiptoed past a scattering of brown boobies seated like statues just above the tide line, upright but fast asleep, heads tucked to their chests, while others still soared overhead in moonlight so bright it cast perfect shadows of flying birds on the sand—and revealed, in the sea, the dark shapes of green turtles waiting offshore. Finally one came in, emerging from the waves with her shell so shiny with seawater that it caught the lunar reflection above, creating the illusion, as she labored up the beach, that she carried the moon on her back. I watched as she slowly dug a hole with her flippers—and disappeared inside to lay her eggs. In the moonlight I could see sprays of sand down the beach, where other greens were preparing nests. We watched into the hours before dawn as turtles came ashore and melted back into the waves, driven up from the sea by the instinct of a species that dates back 175 million years. Feeling privileged to witness so ancient a scene, we were transfixed by the secret night world.

Coasting along through gentle seas the following day, we homed in on Broome—and assessed the Kimberley coast's toll on *Dawn Star II:* One engine was dead, the generator was failing, the refrigeration system had quit, the radio had stopped working, both dinghies were out of commission, and we were down to our last drops of diesel. It was dark by the time we reached Broome, and as we waited at the dock for a lift, looking like shipwreck victims as we sat on our gear, a young tourist couple in matching white shorts and shirts strolled by and asked Eric where we had come from. When he told them "Wyndham," they seemed interested and asked if he would be making the journey again soon. "Not if I can help it," Eric replied with a laugh. "This was a one-time trip."

At the end of Tasman's voyage of 1644, the Dutch officials in Java who had sponsored his trip expressed a bit of disappointment. "What there is in this South-land . . . ," they wrote, "continues unknown, since the men have done nothing beyond sailing along the coast. . . ." While I could empathize with Tasman in his choice to keep sailing, like the officials in Java I yearned to see what lay inland. To complete the circle through the Kimberley, and our imaginary loop back through time, Mike Osborn, his fiancée, Anne Wakelin, and I mapped an overland route back to Wyndham that would take us across the Kimberley plateau, through backcountry that still shelters wilderness raw enough to summon a sense of the oldest view of the land—that of its first explorers, the Aborigines who arrived on the Kimberley shores some 50 millennia before Tasman.

Much of the coastal area we had just traveled was high and dry in the Ice Age, when the ancestors of the Aborigines reached Australia from Southeast Asia, coming south from Indonesia by raft to nearby coasts like the Kimberley, or voyaging east to New Guinea, where they crossed a broad land bridge down to the island continent. It may have been the stark power of the Australian landscape—so bleakly different from the steamy volcanism of island Asia—or it may have arisen, in part, from beliefs they carried with them, but the newcomers in Australia gradually fashioned a mythology as conceptually beautiful as any on earth—and one that offers some notion of the ancient ones' view of their newfound world.

In the beginning, the Dreamtime, when the world was shadowy and formless, totemic ancestors emerged from the earth and came down from the sky to wander the land, calling out names to every rock and spring, every creature and flower, and in naming them, gave them existence. The meandering paths they each followed, singing the world into creation, became known as the "song lines," and in the traditional view, the entire continent is crisscrossed with such musical trails. The memories of those paths and of the deeds of the ancestors have been passed along orally through generations, through millennia, so that many are still known to Aborigines now. One who follows a song line, as if on a sacred pilgrimage, recognizes each creation that links the way and, in retracing the journey and acknowledging what is found, re-creates his world.

As early as 30,000 years ago, people began to engrave and paint sheltered rocks and caves with images symbolizing the ancestral tales. In the Kimberley, so long inhabited by various Aboriginal groups, hidden places in the remote hills and gorges are colorful with galleries of rock art, some in a primitive style perhaps many thousands of years old, some showing the more recent and mysteriously alluring haloed figures known as Wandjinas, spirits that hold the power of lightning and storms and the great floods of the Wet. Unique to the Kimberley, the Wandjinas were revealed to the outside world by the long-ago dreamer George Grey, who happened upon caves of Wandjina paintings in the Prince Regent region. Since then, archaeologists and others roaming the land have continued to find new art sites—some still held sacred, others long forgotten—and we planned to look for them along the way as we set off from Broome to follow our own modern song line across the Kimberley.

We still rocked inside with the rhythms of the sea as we rolled briefly down the Kimberley's main highway, a smooth bitumen road first paved in 1987 that skirts the region in an arc from Broome to Wyndham. Turning off to the town of Derby, we headed northeast on the Gibb River Road, the lone artery across the Kimberley interior—a bone-rattling, four-wheel-drive, washboard dirt track that is only passable in the Dry. It was built sometime after the turn of the century for driving cattle to port at Wyndham and Derby; for despite earlier European failures, some settlement finally came to the Kimberley in the form of cattlemen and sheepmen who pushed into the land from east and west in the late 1800s. The cattle survived, and today about two-thirds of the Kimberley is divided up and leased out in stations, huge ranches that average a thousand square miles—nearly the size of Rhode Island—but that are so big and untamed that even the station land is basically a wilderness, with cows.

At first we crossed a country of plains as long and lonely as the American West, complete with widely spread herds of cattle, but they grazed among ranks and rows of termite mounds—tall, spired fingers and huge, mud-mound heaps—in fields sprinkled with fantastical, African-style baobabs, the emblem tree of the Kimberley. Known as "boabs" in Australia, the trees are related to the seven other species of baobab found only in Africa and Madagascar, and scientists speculate that their seeds floated ashore some 75 million years ago, after Australia had broken off and begun to drift east from the old southern supercontinent of Gondwanaland. The trees took root in the Kimberley region, where they remain unique. With their great swollen trunks and fingerlike branches, each seems a character that has struck its own pose. Every one seems so expressive of a human stance and emotion—some joyous and up-reaching, some bent with the blues, others grouped together in lively gatherings—that traveling past them is like recognizing people you know.

Farther inland we journeyed back to the days of Gondwanaland, when the Kimberley coast reappeared to us in an ancient form. Just off the Gibb River Road we rounded a bend to meet the sheer limestone ramparts of the Oscar and Napier Ranges, jagged remnants of a former great barrier reef that edged the shores of northwestern Australia 360 million years ago. In several places lovely streams—raging rivers in the Wet—have cut gorges through the reef's high walls, and we followed a path through one to a secluded cave in the back of the Napier Range where a huge red Wandjina stared down at us.

A halo of rays fanned out from its face, painted white with haunting, hollow red eyes. Surrounding it were red figures with outstretched fingers—other Wandjinas whose eyes and haloes had faded. Nearby were painted two white crocodiles side by side, and two pale snakes were near its feet. In Dreamtime mythology legions of pythons slithered into the land from the east, carving the Kimberley's rivers and gorges as they traveled down to the sea. Stories of Wandjinas tell of complicated migrations of different tribes of the spirits, culminating in a great battle of Wandjinas in the central Kimberley, after which they all wandered off into caves and, leaving their physical forms as painted images on the rocks, changed into spirits with far-reaching powers. Like certain animals, including snakes and crocodiles, Wandjinas control the spirits of children-to-be, who live in river pools like the ones below the Wandjina cave, and when a man passes by, one may enter him, appear in his dreams, and be transferred to the mother-to-be. At birth the child is named for its Wandjina, and at the end of life a man's remains may be placed near the source of his child spirit. We stared back at the tall, haloed figure, its bright colors indicating a fairly recent repainting—a traditional ritual that keeps the Wandjina alive. On a rock ledge nearby I found a small pile of bones rubbed with red ocher—someone returned to his spirit's home.

We camped among the boabs near the old reef that night, sleeping in the canvas bed-rolls Australians call swags under the stars in the cold night air. In the morning we jittered off north up the Gibb River Road, crossing over range after range of rough, red hills, through miles of gum forests and golden savannas, stopping here and there for billabong swims, hiking along rivers and into deep gorges, in a land where the sun broils the rocks to red griddles and so steadily saps the strength from your muscles that, like mountain climbers at high altitude, you walk ever more slowly, stop ever more often, always scanning for water and shade. The bush flies for which Australia is infamous were, in Mike's words, "exceptionally friendly here," and wherever we hiked, each of us moved in a personal orb of flies—Mike's never defecting to me, or mine to Anne. The flies are a fact of life in the Kimberley wilderness that, like the mosquitoes unseen in a luscious tropical picture, can hardly be imagined from afar. The best that can be said of them is that at least at night, they rest.

We made camps along wild river billabongs where wallabies bounced off and dingoes roamed near and huge cranes flapped by with pterodactyl wingbeats. As we traveled north, we became increasingly intrigued by a place we approached—a shaded area on the map labeled Drysdale River National Park. It covers nearly 1,400 square miles in the north-central Kimberley, and has no facilities or rangers and no roads whatsoever leading into it. With permission to cross station land adjoining the park, we struck off from the road down a disused track and into the bush for a glimpse of the wildest of the Kimberley.

We navigated by the path of the sun and an outdated map through eucalyptus forests, down steep ravines, over fields of black stones, floodplains of boulders, and savannas of dry grass higher than our vehicle's hood—where we encountered a few startled wild horses—finally reaching a bluff over the shallows of the Carson River, the boundary of the park. Across the river rose a magnificent escarpment, an orange wall reaching heights of a thousand feet and stretching the length of the river to the north and south, and darkened, up high, with deep ledges and the black eyes of caves. We made camp on the riverbank, taking an evening swim in a billabong shining with the red eyes of freshies.

In the morning we contemplated the wall before us, trying to imagine what places might have once been sacred, choosing to climb to a spot under a cave and explore. The hiking was hard—over fallen boulders and prickly spinifex grass, through thorny scrub and tangled trees up steep scree slopes—but we stayed our course to the spot we had chosen, and when we reached it, we found paintings. There were white bird tracks, a creature that looked like a turtle—and one very faded Wandjina. Nearby we found more, a lovely pale gallery of red animals—kangaroos, lizards, a snake and an emu, a frog, and a jabiru bird—all painted in an early primitive style similar to that found across northern Australia. For two days we hiked the escarpment, choosing destinations up the wall where we imagined rock art might be. To our astonishment we found paintings at each place we reached—as if we had conjured them into existence. Much later, when I asked scientists at the Western Australian Museum in Perth if the paintings we found were recorded, they informed me that the area was so under-explored that our finds were probably new, and when Mike eventually took photographs of the paintings to people in several Aboriginal communities, no one knew them any longer, their tales had been lost. Of all that we found, the elegant creatures, abstract shapes and tracks, one stands in my mind above all, a motif common to rock-art sites all over Australia, painted on the wall near the faded Wandjina. It was a simple human handprint, colored in red, the mark of an individual soul, a poignant declaration of self at one small place in a vast old land.

We headed back down the road toward Wyndham, passing hills and valleys, lone rocks and bouldered slopes, shattered plains of stones, broken like glass, dotted with gums and kapoks and boabs, thinking of every feature as having been sung into existence in the imaginations of the first Aborigines, and hearing, in our own minds, a music in the land. The song was soothing, like sweet strings where the wind rushes in cool gusts through paperbarks by the billabongs; but it was low and mournful through the plains of hot boulders, an unceasing dirge through fields of sunburnt grass, low and buzzing like flies droning in the heat, with no break in breath until bells chime in for the yellow kapok blossoms and the flocks of orange lorikeets flitting past in the sun. In the distance we saw the rose-colored buttes of Wyndham's Cockburn Range, their slopes skinned and lean like the sinews of a wild animal, encircled up high with a band of orange rock, a long python coiling the hills. On the hot plains below, wavering with mirage, the boabs seemed to dance, receiving us at the end of our song line through a land where you can still follow the tracks of the old ones, and sing out a world of your own.

Sea cave walls preserve Aboriginal paintings on Bigge Island in the Bonaparte Archipelago. The sailing ship and helmeted figure with pipe may depict the arrival of Europeans as early as the 17th century.

FOLLOWING PAGES: Foaming tidal water cleaves treacherous outcrops corrugated by erosion in Secure Bay. Kimberley tides rise and fall as much as 40 feet, creating chains of whirlpools.

DAVID DOUBILET (OPPOSITE AND FOLLOWING PAGES)

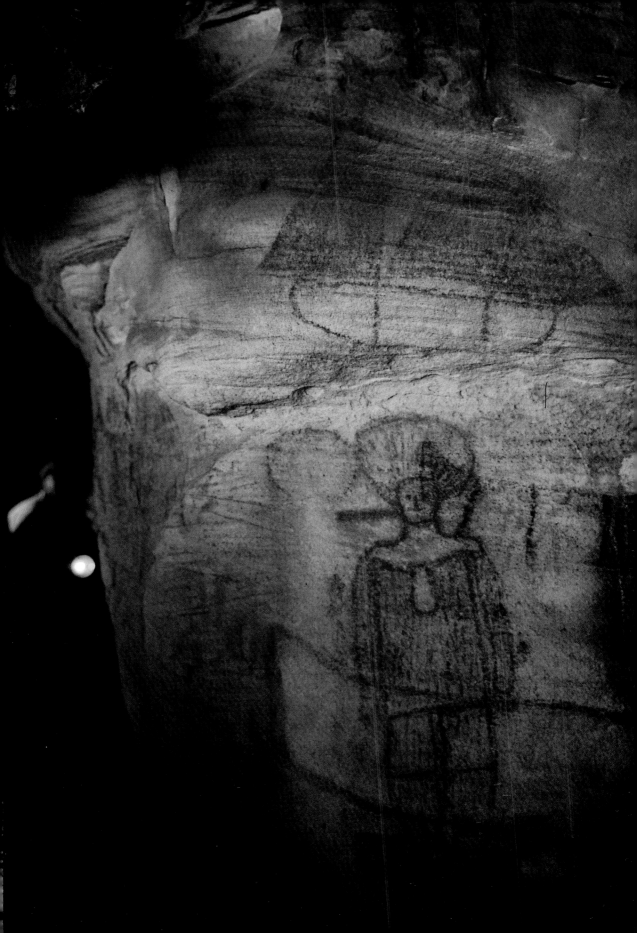

*R*apacious reptiles from the age of dinosaurs, saltwater crocodiles patrol the Kimberley's tidal rivers and coastal wetlands. "Salties" can weigh more than a ton and reach lengths of 20 feet. Short legs and ponderous belly make the agile creatures look sluggish on land. With a sudden lash of jaws the crocs can snatch low-flying birds from the air. Nervously aware that they are easy game for these Australian man-eaters, the author and guide Mike Osborn hurry to free their skiff from the mud in a small tributary of the Prince Regent River. In 1987 a saltie attacked and killed an American tourist at nearby King Cascade.

FOLLOWING PAGES: Muddied by tidal silt, the King River buckles into an oxbow. The watercourse meanders through salt marshes to the West Arm inlet of Cambridge Gulf near Wyndham town.

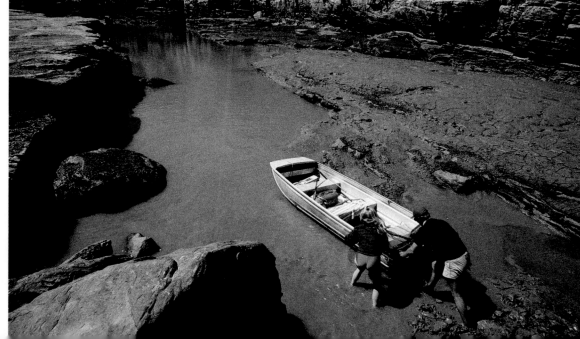

With *aerobatic aplomb, a galah alights. In the 1800s this species, the rose-breasted cockatoo, provided the main ingredient for "parrot pies," a survival food of Australia's settlers. Strong fliers, the 14-inch-long birds range throughout most of the Australian mainland.*

*S*urrounded by a sea of cane and buffle grass, Mike Osborn searches for the best route back
to the Great Northern Highway near the town of Derby. Hours of exploring the flooded backcountry
south of King Sound left Mike's four-wheel-drive Land Cruiser mud splattered.

FOLLOWING PAGES: A wispy veil of moisture trails from thunderheads near the Mitchell Plateau
in the Kimberley's far north. Three months of heavy rain each year allow the seasonal lushness of this
rugged and little explored region, which harbors an abundance of wildlife south of Admiralty Gulf.

*R*adiant in late afternoon sun, the sandstone bulwarks of King George Falls brighten a treeless plain that reaches to the Timor Sea on the Kimberley's northern coast (above). Its roots a living vein in sandstone, a rock fig makes a long reach between sky and soil (opposite). The slender tree, Ficus platypoda, *flourishes in harsh settings and bears a tasty fruit prized by the Kimberley's Aborigines and favored by bats. More than 50 different kinds of figs grow throughout the continent.*

Clawlike cliffs grip the grassland of Purnululu National Park in the Bungle Bungle Range. Some 350 million years of erosion carved this escarpment of stratified rocks, beehive-shaped towers, and dead-end gorges. A national park since 1987, the area presents an outstanding display of banded sandstone.

FOLLOWING PAGES: "God planted the baobab upside down with its roots in the air," according to a legend; a bloated trunk, packed with water-storage tissue, rises from a Kimberley savanna.

*O*utback pharmacy: A termite mound provides bush medicine for Aborigine
David Mowaljarli. After collecting bits of soil that he chips from the mound, he will mix
the fine debris with water. Aborigines drink the elixir to cure intestinal ailments.

"Smoking the baby," Aborigine Rita Sturt passes her infant granddaughter Veronica through pungent fumes. She and the infant's mother and great-grandmother built the ritual fire and smothered it with green leaves of a conkerberry bush to produce the scented vapors. The smoke, Aborigines believe, clears a newborn's chest and head and gives the child a healthy start in life.

*A*boriginal elders prepare for a corroboree, an Aboriginal ritual of songs and dances.
One man "paints up" with crushed white ocher (below). Behind him a fellow elder plays
a didgeridoo, a trumpetlike musical instrument made of wood or bamboo.
Corroborees recall the Dreamtime, a mythical era when spirit beings shaped the earth's features.
Opposite, an Aboriginal performer readies himself for another festival.

FOLLOWING PAGES: Specters known as Wandjina figures appear to float like clouds
in this display of Aboriginal rock art discovered on cave walls near the Kimberley's Gibb River.

NGS PHOTOGRAPHER SAM ABELL (OPPOSITE)

Notes on Contributors

The Muli assignment sent free-lancer JEFFREY AARONSON on his 19th photographic foray into China since 1980. Working out of Aspen, Colorado, he has traveled the world shooting for such leading publications as *Time, Vogue,* and *Paris Match.*

Born of American parents in Beirut, Lebanon, PATRICK BOOZ grew up in Pakistan and Indonesia and earned a degree in Asian studies at the University of Wisconsin. He combines his writing skills with fluency in three Chinese dialects.

PAUL CHESLEY has handled a diversity of photographic assignments for the Society's books and magazines over the past 20 years. He is a founder of Photographers/Aspen, Inc., a photo agency in Aspen, Colorado, his present residence.

Free-lance photographer JAY DICKMAN lives in Littleton, Colorado. For 16 years he shot pictures as a staffer on the *Dallas Times Herald* in his home state of Texas. His coverage of political turmoil in El Salvador won him the Pulitzer Prize for feature photography in 1983.

CHRISTINE ECKSTROM turned free-lance writer after 16 years with the Society. Wide-ranging assignments have taken her from America's Atlantic isles to the world's grasslands. She has also written the Special Publication entitled *Forgotten Edens.*

Veteran staff member TOM MELHAM has written about the world's natural wonders for nearly 30 years. He has roamed from arctic wilderness to coral reef. He reports that few locales rival Venezuela's "Lost World" of "broken rockscapes, unique plants, Indian legends, and tales of living dinosaurs."

THOMAS O'NEILL joined the Society in 1976. He is the author of *Back Roads America* and *Lakes, Peaks, and Prairies,* as well as chapters in many other Special Publications. He is now on the writing staff of NATIONAL GEOGRAPHIC magazine and has written about such topics as the Mekong River and the Australian Dog Fence.

CYNTHIA RUSS RAMSAY paid her second visit to Timbuktu for the Mali chapter. She first wrote about the fabled African city in *Nature on the Rampage.* Other Special Publications that carry her accounts of faraway places include *Nature's World of Wonders, The Emerald Realm,* and *Excursion to Enchantment.*

Photojournalist MAGGIE STEBER has won many awards recording the saga of human struggle, notably in Africa, Haiti, and Cuba. Her career in free-lance photography began in 1978, when she left a picture-editing post in New York to cover guerrilla warfare in Zimbabwe.

Acknowledgments

The Book Division is grateful to the individuals, groups, and organizations named or quoted in the text and to those cited here for their assistance during the production of this Special Publication: Freddy Barreat, Paul Berry, Herman Beÿerbergen, CECOMA-MARAVEN, Francisco Delascio Chitty, Salmana Cisse, Tom Givnish, Jorge M. Gonzalez, Marsha Haynes, Peter Klika, Roy McDiarmid, Burnett and Mimi Miller, Robin E. Poulton, Jean-René Rinfret, Herman Róo, Peter P. Strzok, Kathy Tilford, Venezuelan Air Force, Eugen Wehrli, Franz Weibezahn.

Additional Reading

Readers may wish to consult the *National Geographic Index* for related articles and books. The following books may be of special interest.

Muli: Joseph F. Rock, *The Ancient Na-Khi Kingdom of Southwest China;* Morris Rossabi, *Khubilai Khan;* R. A. Stein, *Tibetan Civilization.*

Mali: E. W. Bovill, *The Golden Trade of the Moors* (2nd ed.); Brian Gardner, *The Quest for Timbuctoo;* Christopher Lloyd, *The Search for The Niger;* Kim Naylor, *Discover Guide to West Africa: The Niger and Gambia River Route;* Stephen Pern, *The Dogon: Masked Dancers of West Africa.*

Iceland: Ulrich Münzer, *Iceland: Volcanoes, Glaciers, Geysers;* Katharine Scherman, *Daughter of Fire: A Portrait of Iceland;* Deanna Swaney, *Iceland, Greenland & the Faroe Islands.*

Venezuela: Charles Brewer-Carías, *Roraima: The Crystal Mountain;* Tom Cahill, *The Lost World;* L. R. Dennison, *Devil Mountain;* David Nott, *Into the Lost World;* Lark Weidmann, *La Grand Sabana.*

Australia: I. M. Crawford, *The Art of the Wandjina;* Ron & Viv Moon, *The Kimberley: An Adventurer's Guide;* Michael and Irene Morcombe, *Discover Australia's National Parks & Naturelands;* Reader's Digest, *Wild Australia* (2nd ed.); Tony Wheeler, *Australia: A Travel Survival Kit;* G. Arnold Wood, *The Discovery of Australia.*

Index

Boldface indicates illustrations.

Library of Congress CIP Data
Beyond the horizon : adventures in faraway lands / prepared by the
   Book Division, National Geographic Society.
         p.   cm.
      Includes bibliographical references and index.
      ISBN 0-87044-831-5
      1. Voyages and travels—1981–   I. National Geographic Society
   (U.S.). Book Division.
   G465.B487   1992
   910.4—dc20   91-44615
                                                            CIP

Composition for this book by the Typographic section of National Geographic Production Services, Pre-Press Division. Set in Berkeley Book. Printed and bound by R. R. Donnelley & Sons, Willard, Ohio. Color separations by Graphic Art Service, Inc., Nashville, Tenn.; Lanman Progressive Co., Washington, D.C.; Lincoln Graphics, Inc., Cherry Hill, N.J. Dust jacket printed by Federated Lithographers-Printers, Inc., Providence, R.I.

The world's largest nonprofit scientific and educational organization, the National Geographic Society was founded in 1888 "for the increase and diffusion of geographic knowledge." Since then it has supported scientific exploration and spread information to its more than nine million members worldwide.

The National Geographic Society educates and inspires millions every day through magazines, books, television programs, videos, maps and atlases, research grants, the National Geography Bee, teacher workshops, and innovative classroom materials.

The Society is supported through membership dues and income from the sale of its educational products. Members receive NATIONAL GEOGRAPHIC magazine— the Society's official journal—discounts on Society products, and other benefits. For more information about the National Geographic Society and its educational programs and publications, please call 1-800-NGS-LINE (647-5463), or write to the following address:

National Geographic Society
1145 17th Street N.W.
Washington, D.C. 20036-4688
U.S.A.

Visit the Society's Web site at
www.nationalgeographic.com